MIWA OGASAWARA
UNSPOKEN

HIRMER

"Ambiguity asks, Where is the border between this and that? Ambiguity does not obey logic [...] ambiguity is inherently contradictory and insoluble, a bewildering truth of fogs and mists and the unrecognizable figure or phantom or memory or dream that cannot be contained or held in my hands because it is always flying away [...]"

Siri Hustvedt

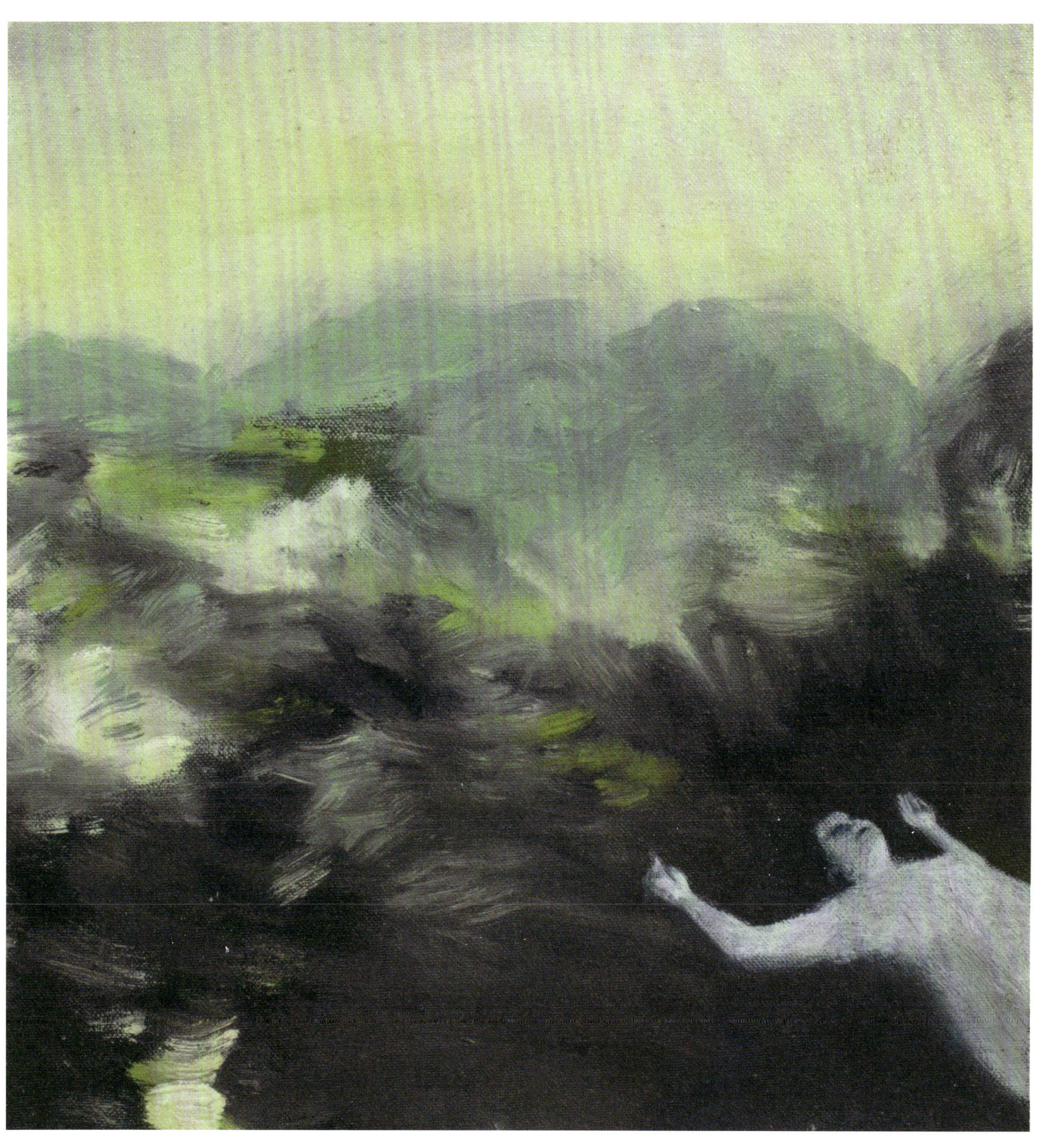

BEGINNING 2004 / 36×34 cm

All paintings: oil on canvas

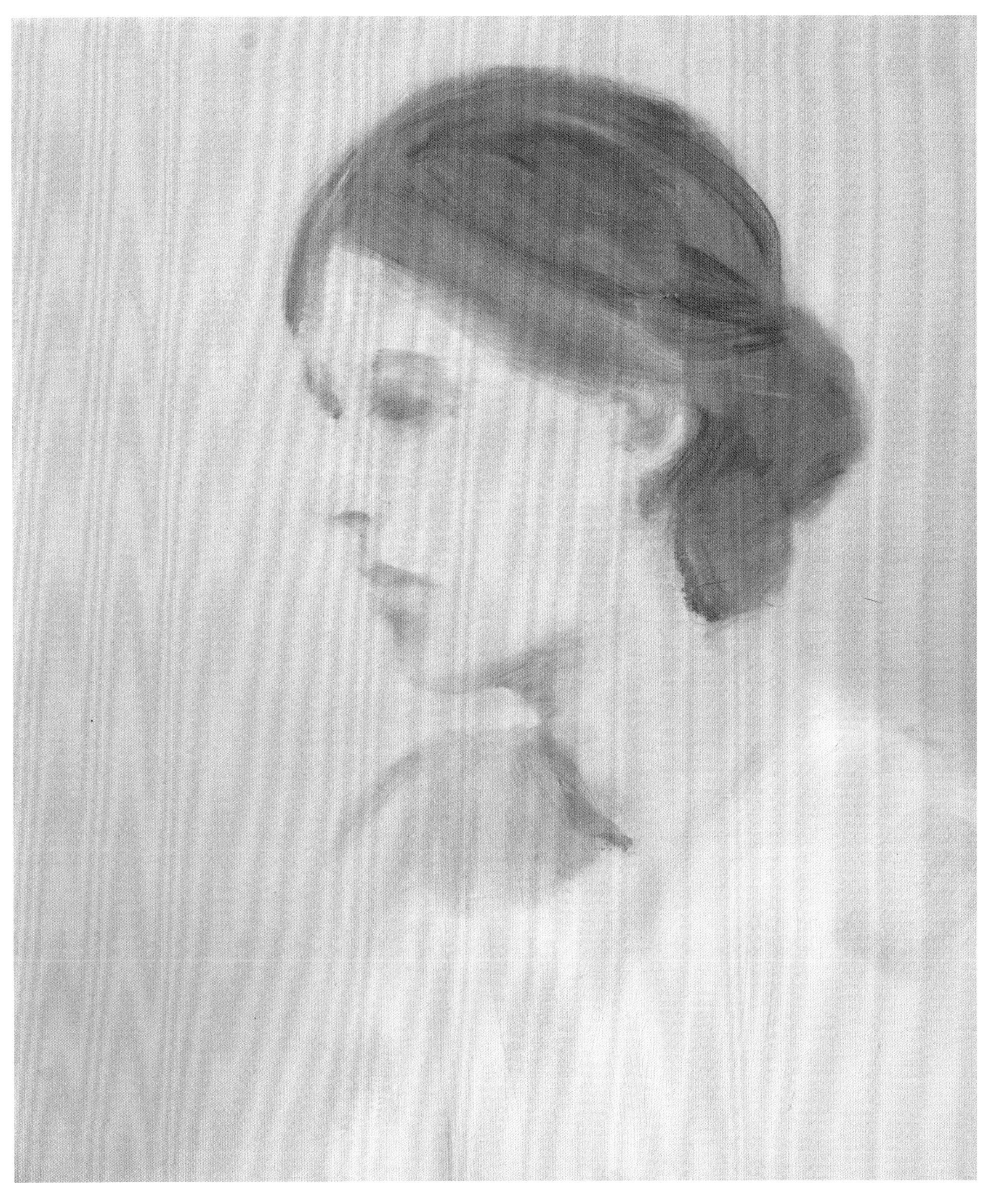

V. W. 2014 / 35×30 cm

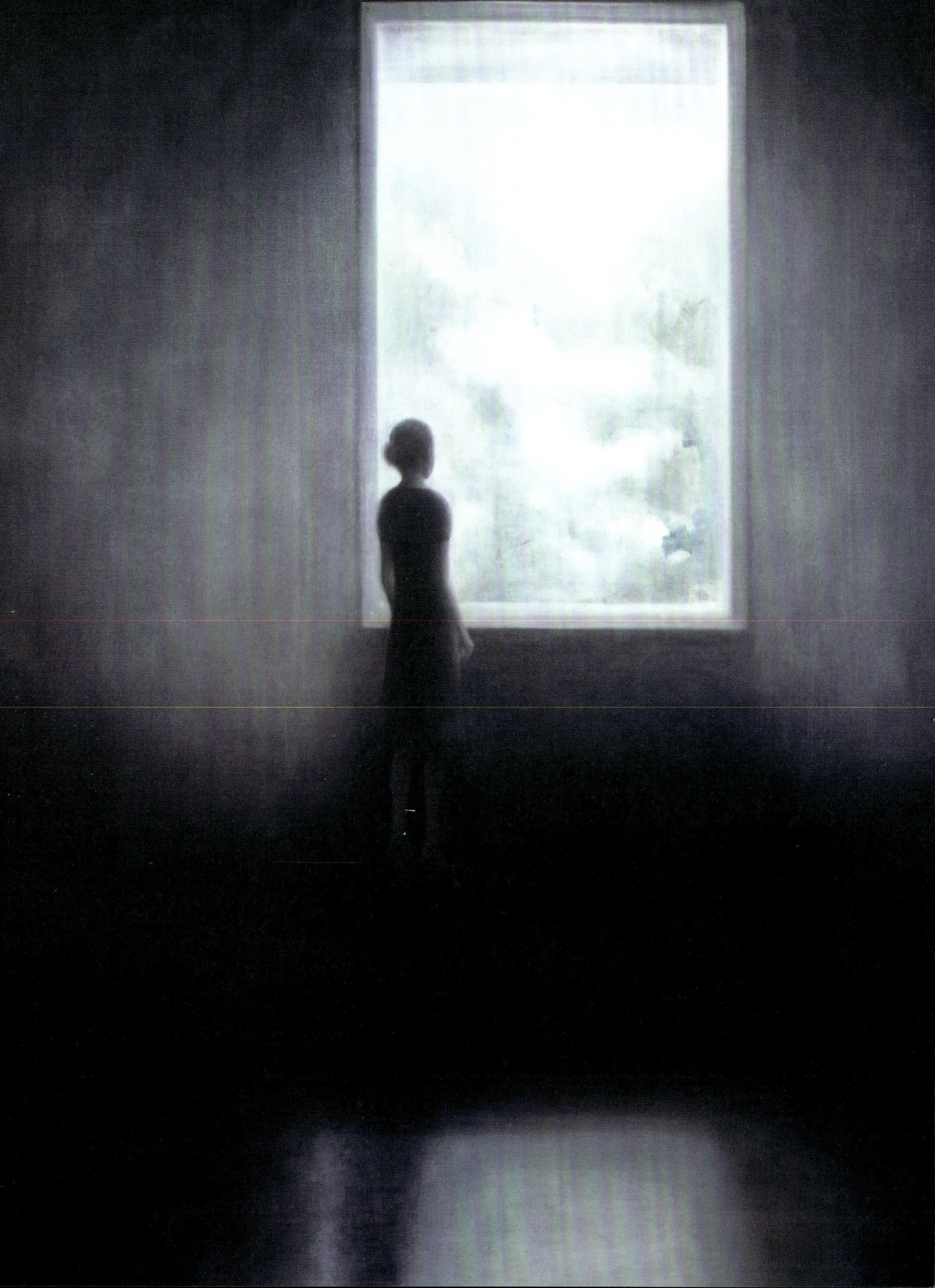

AUS DEM FENSTER 2018 / 200 × 150 cm AM UFER > 2020 / 170 × 230 cm

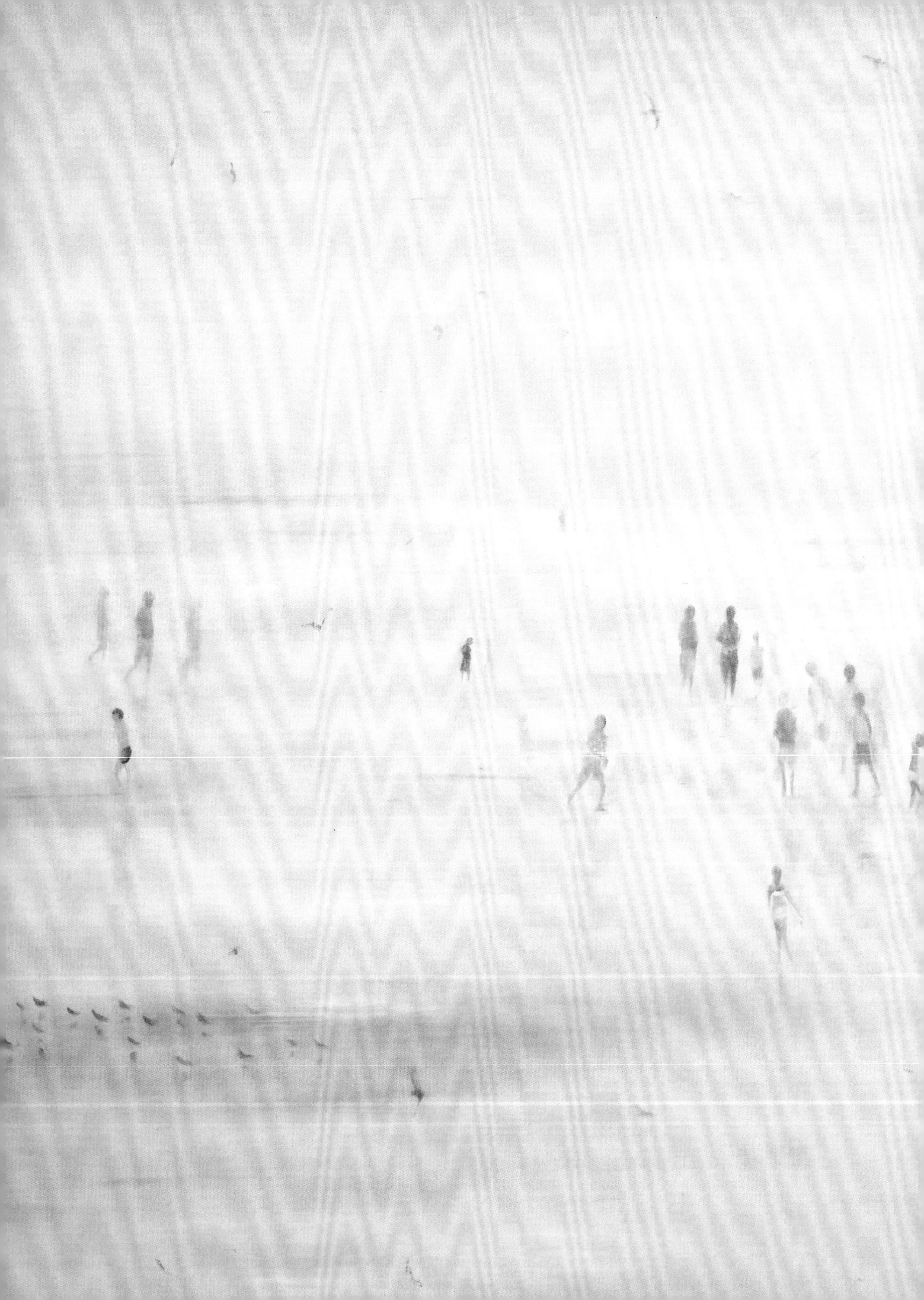

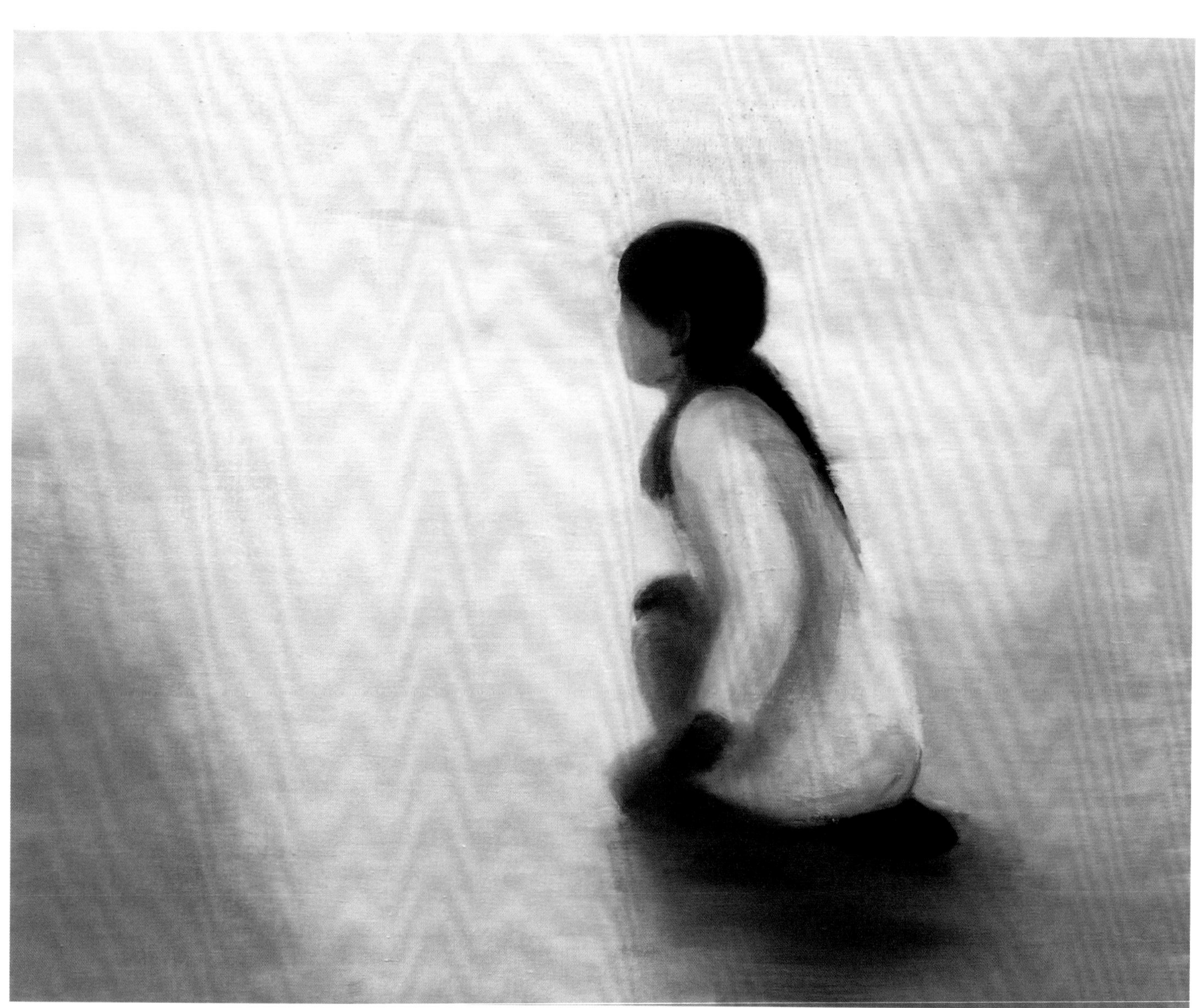

BADEWANNE 2007 / 30 × 30 cm

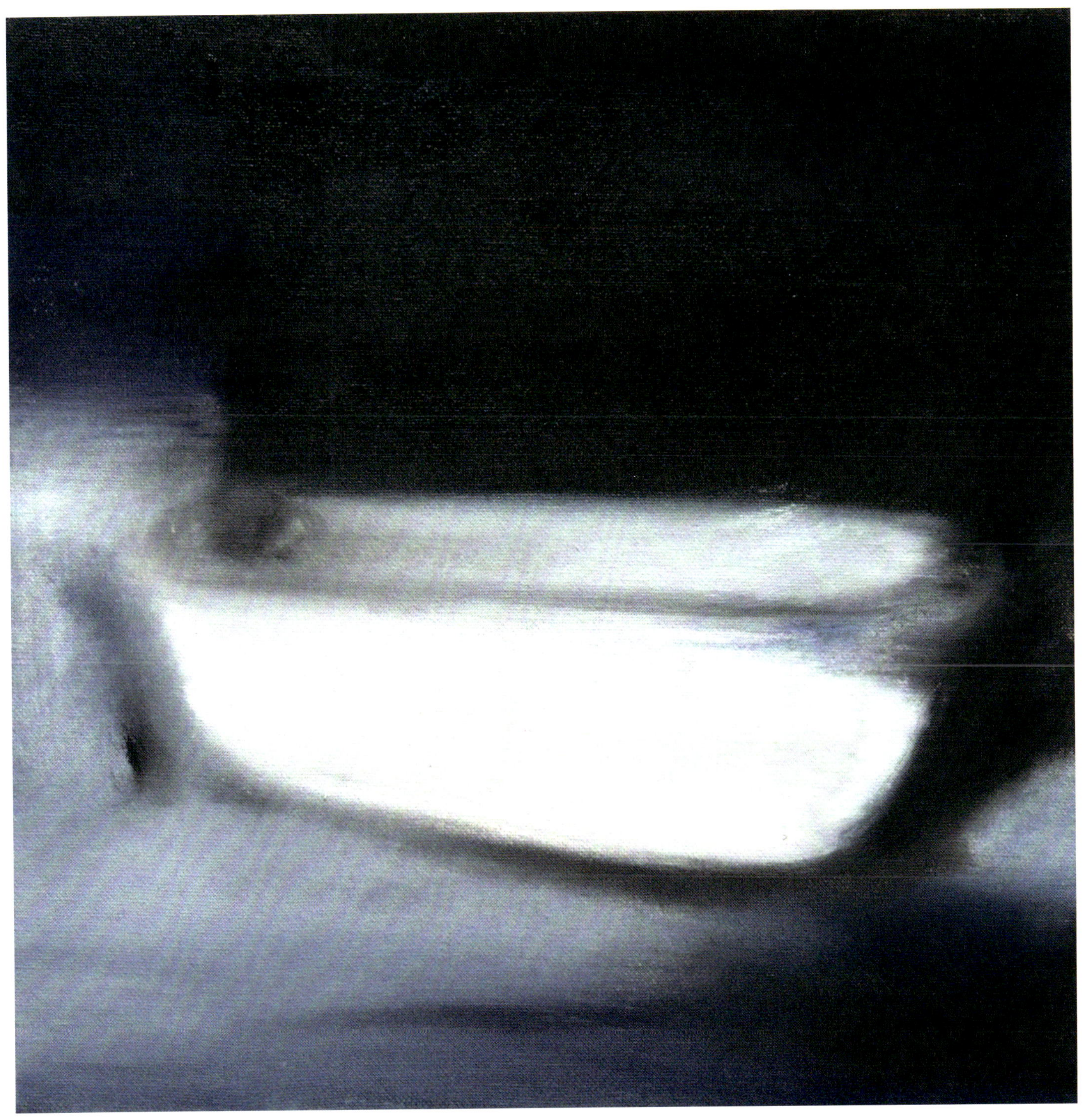

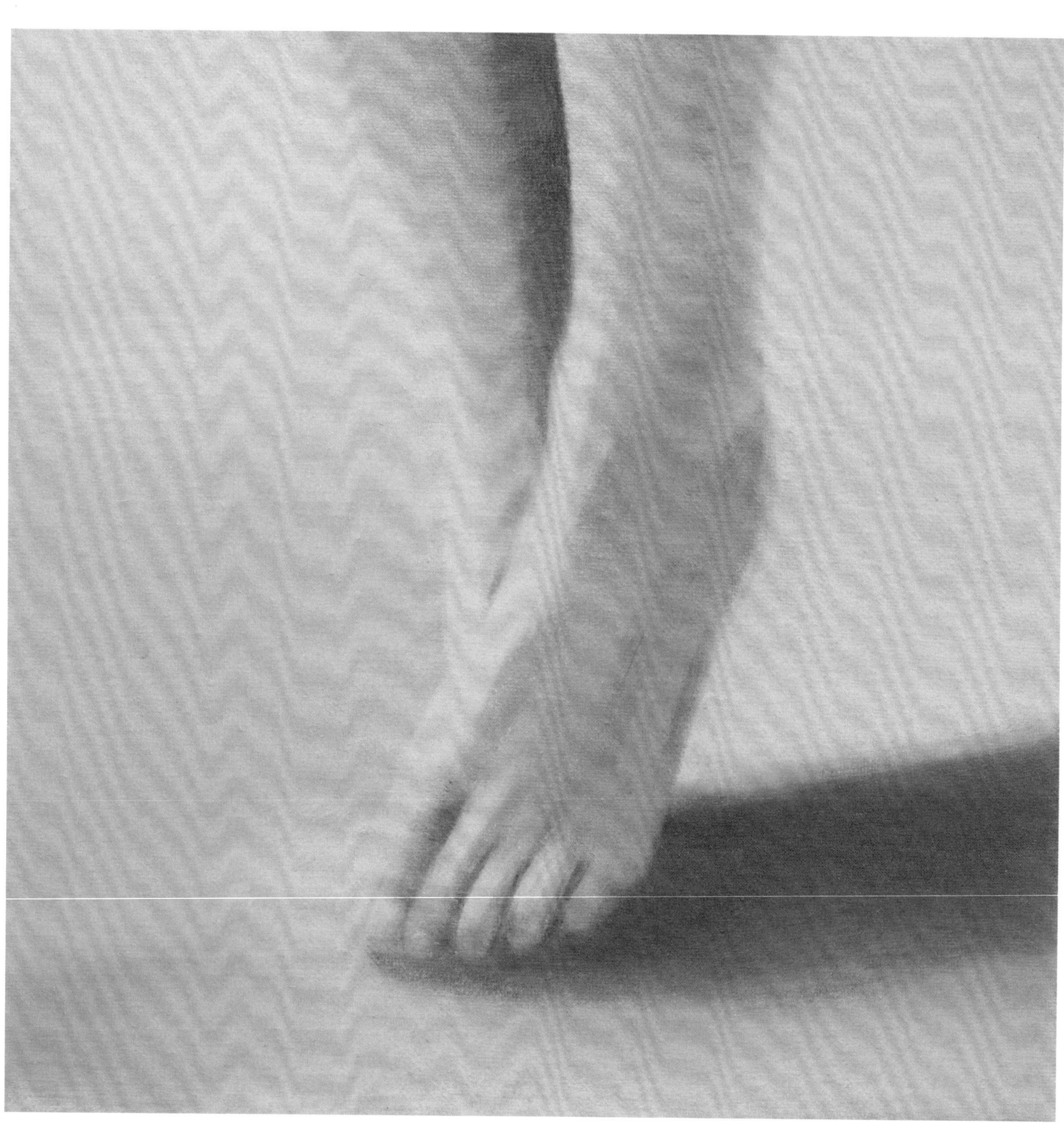

 SKIN 13 2014 / 30×30 cm

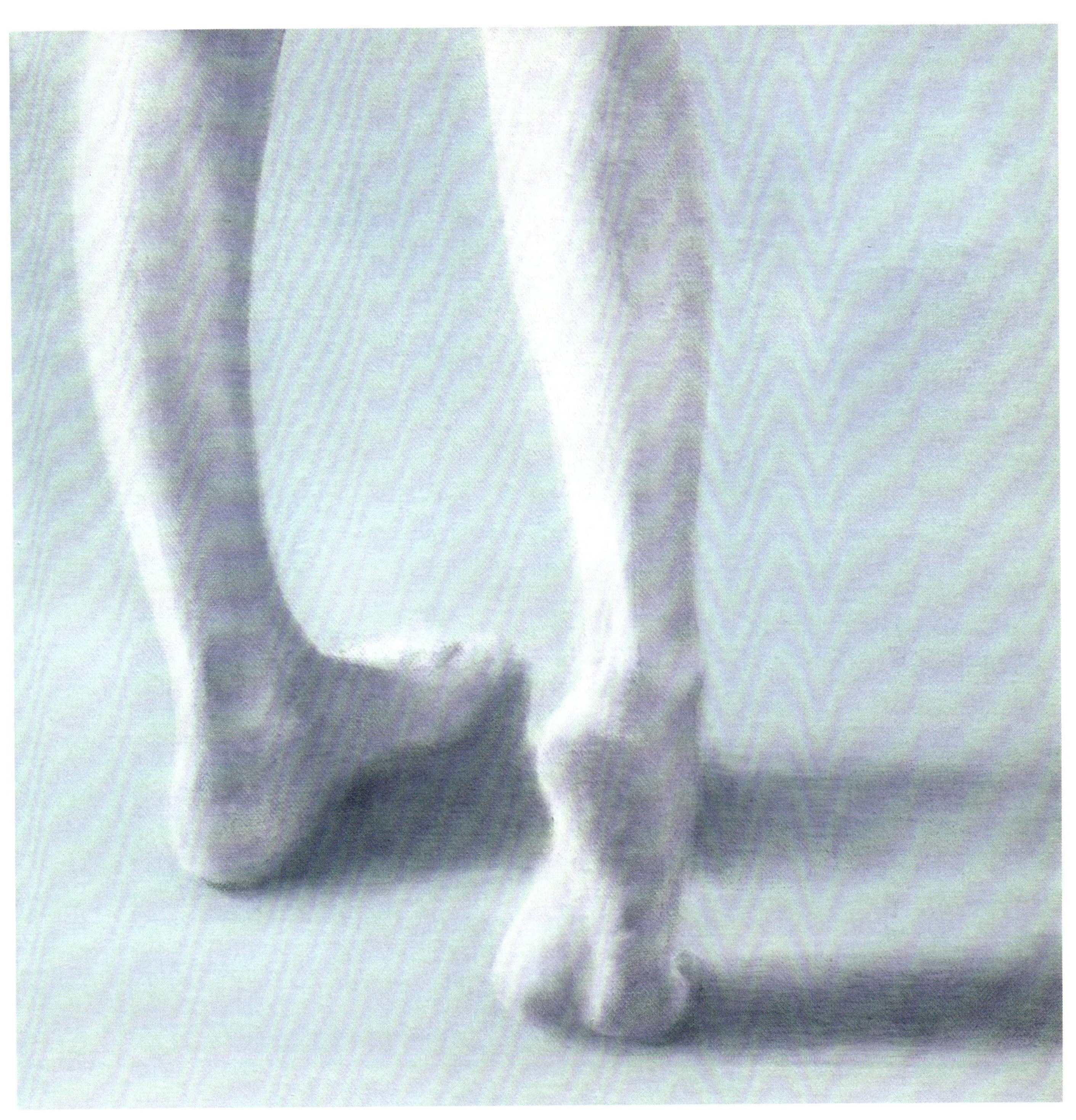

SKIN 11 2011 / 40 × 40 cm

SIMONE 2019 / 35 × 30 cm

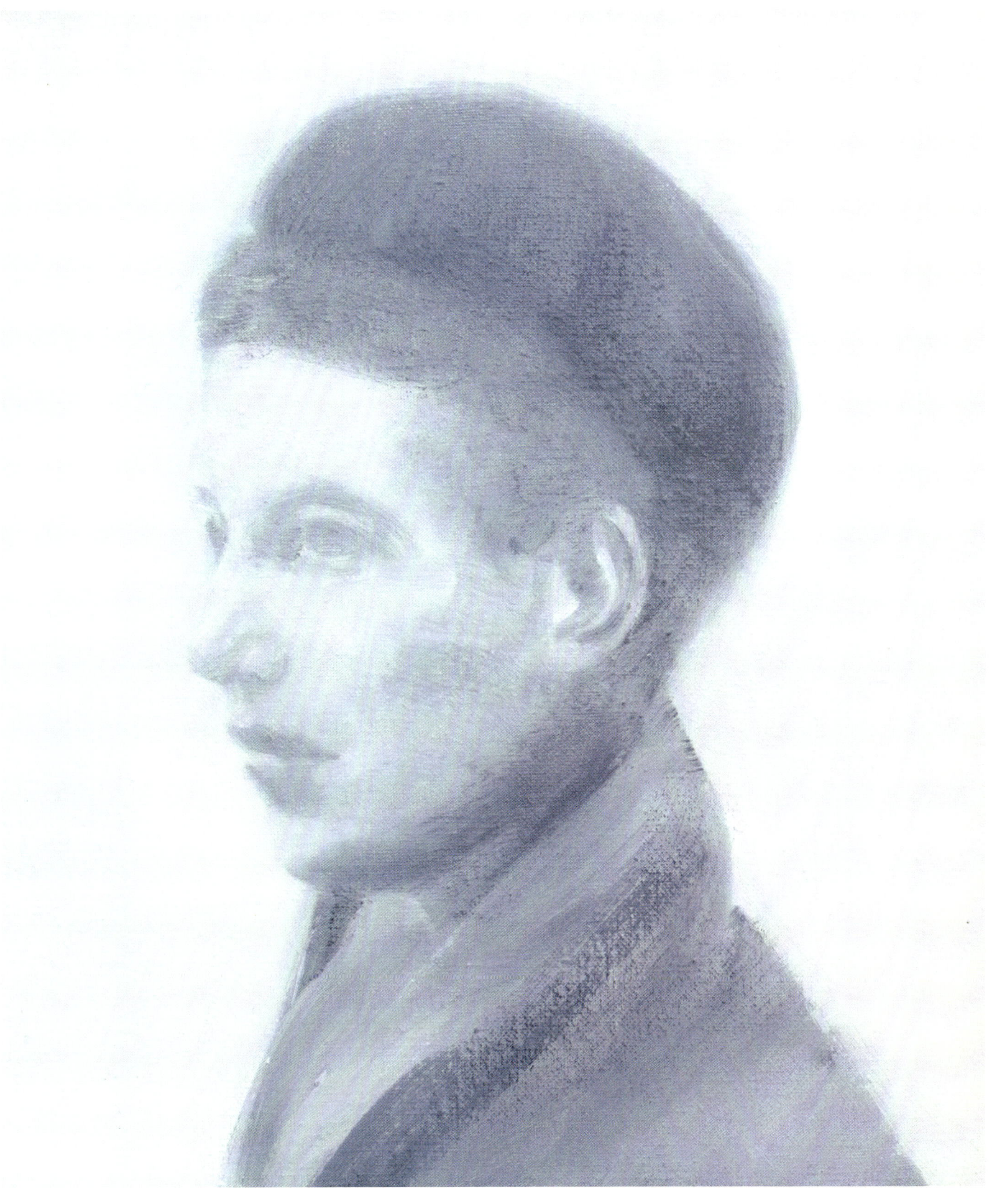

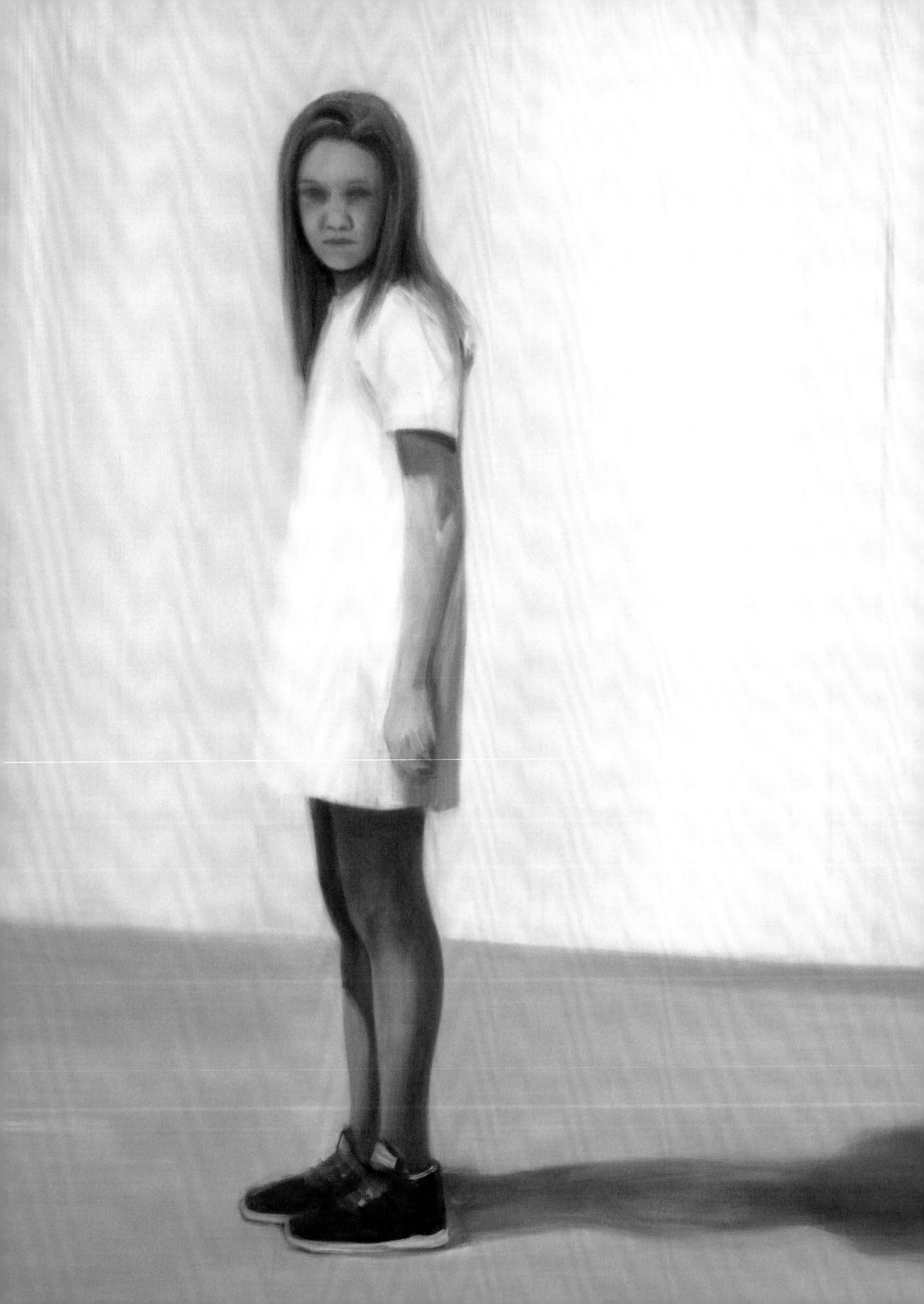

INDIFFERENT 1 2016 / 140 × 160 cm

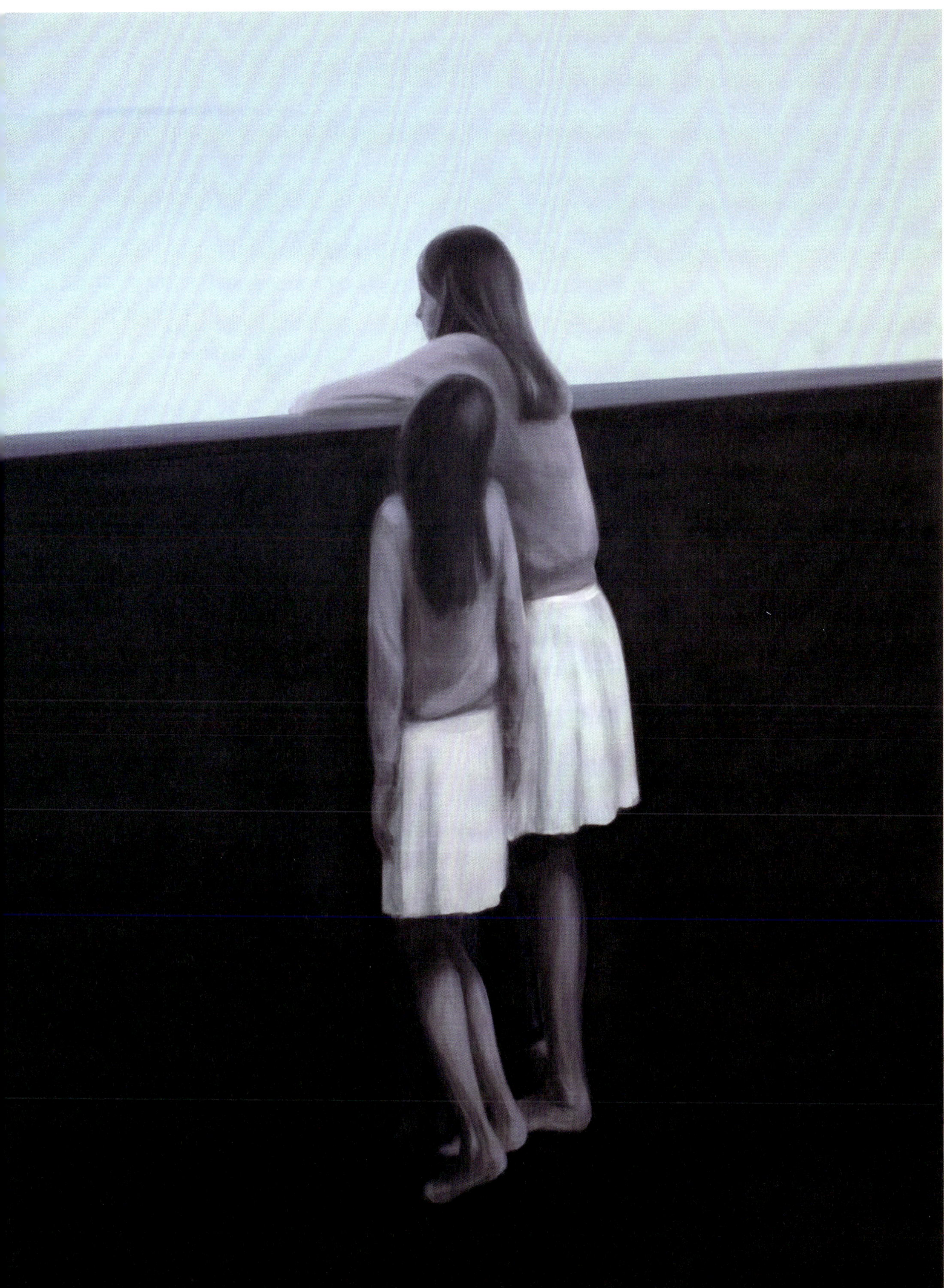

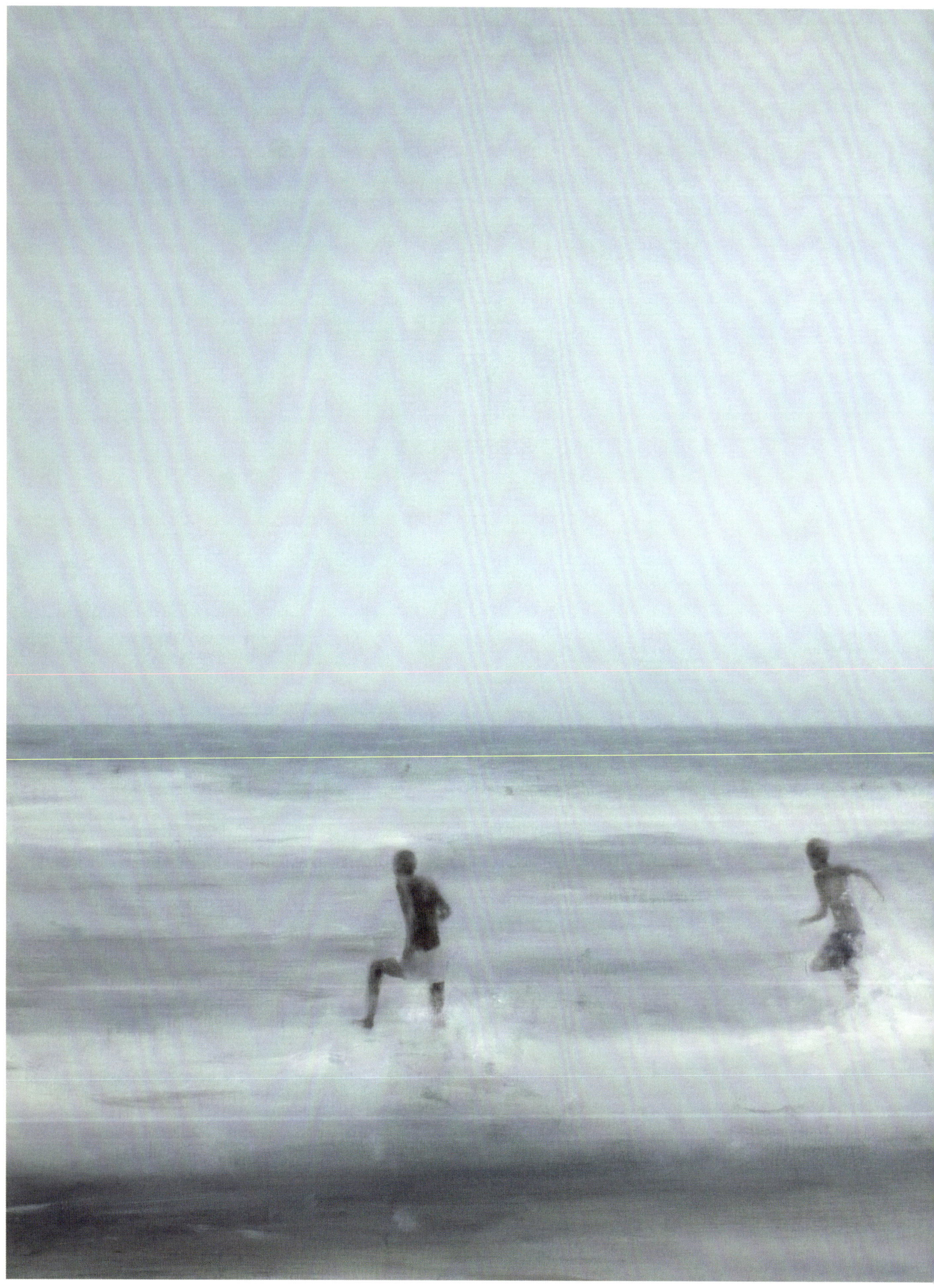

FREED 2019 / 150 × 190 cm

STILLSTAND 2009 / 180 × 150 cm

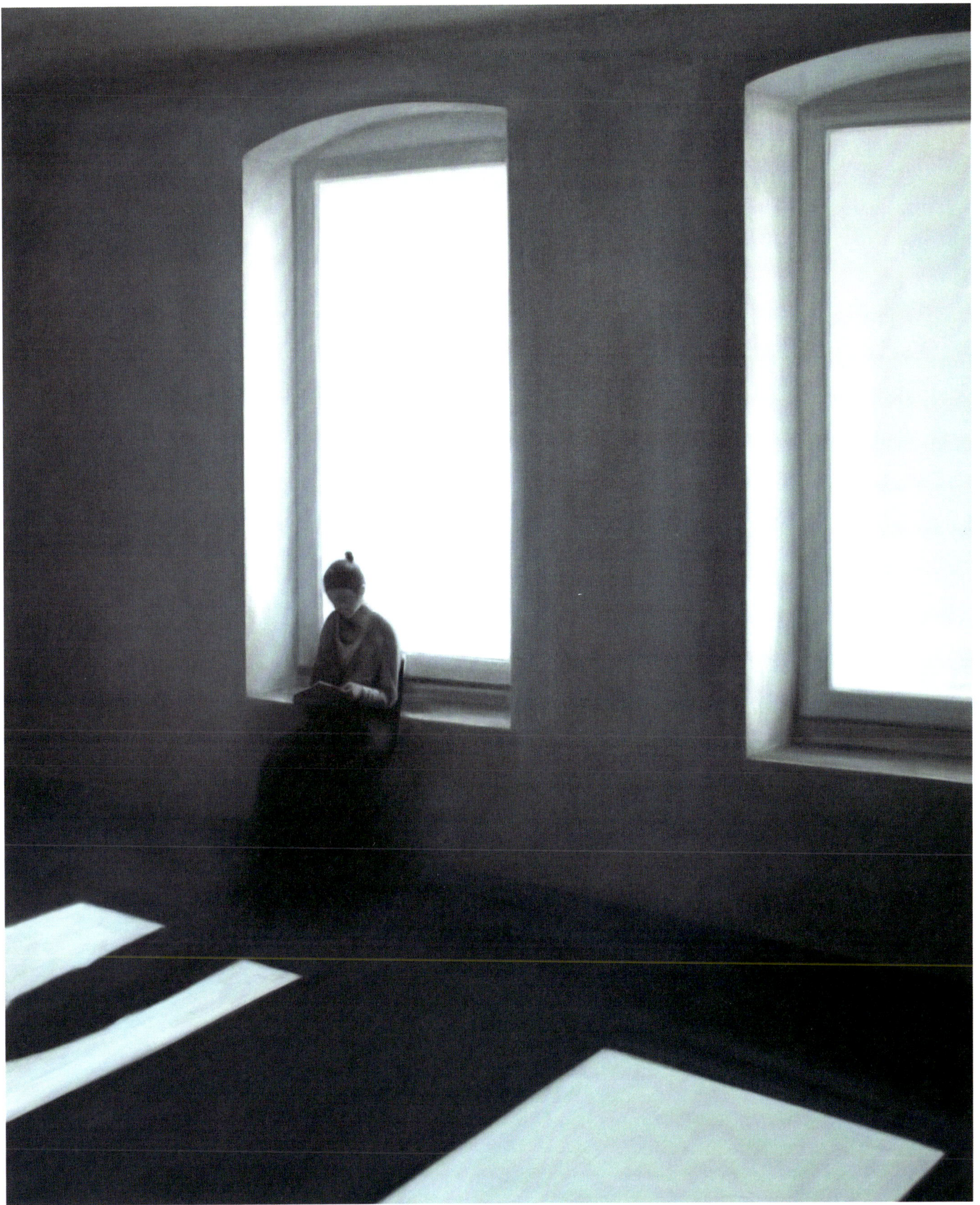

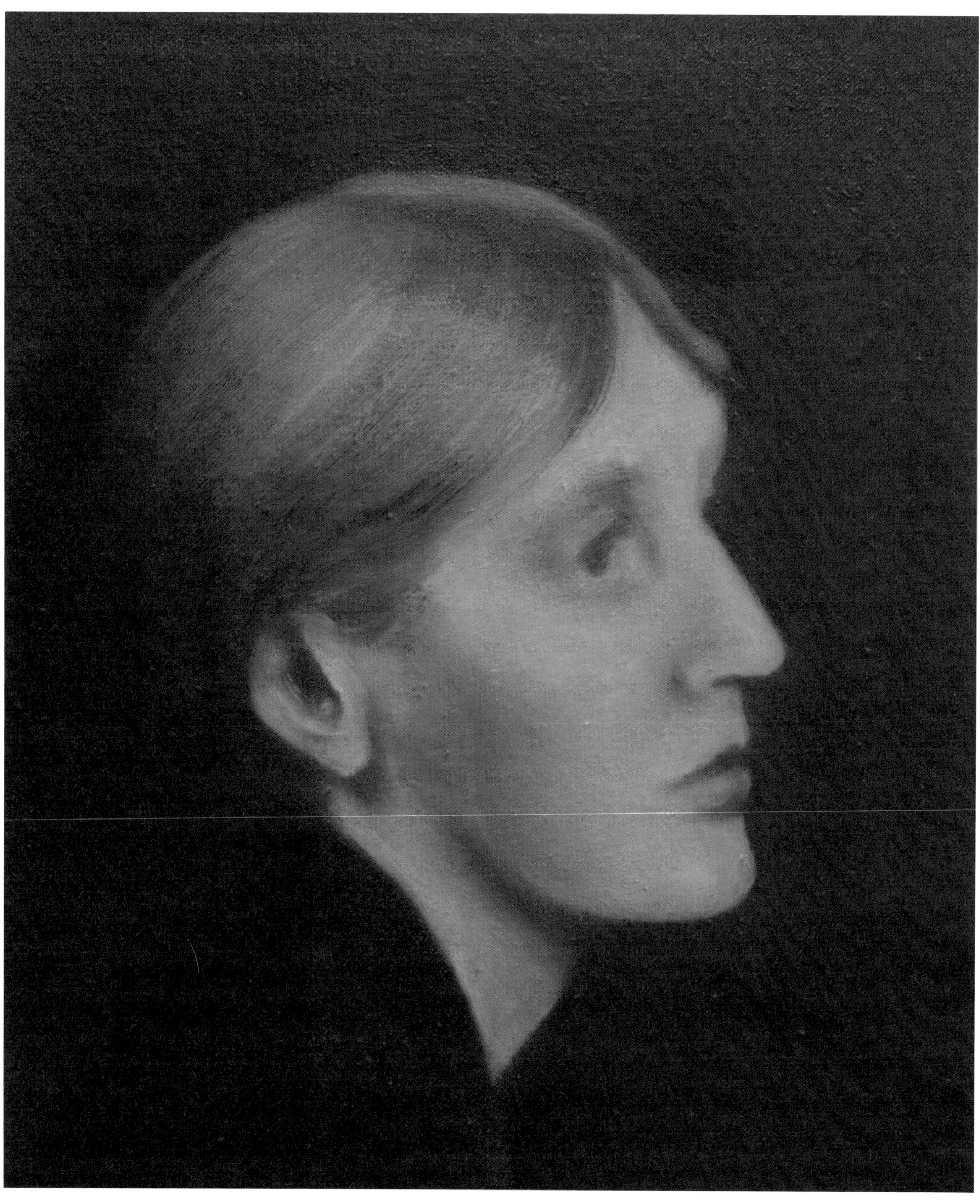

ON THE ATTEMPT TO SEE. THE HUMAN IN THE PICTURE.

NICOLA GRAEF

THE SPECIAL GAZE

It is the gloomy gaze that catches the eye of the observer. A gaze of deep heaviness that seems to lose itself in nothing. This woman appears tired or even exhausted. Weary of life. Yet alert. Having seen all of what life means exhausts you. It is of course no coincidence that Miwa Ogasawara has dedicated several portraits to the English writer Virginia Woolf (1882–1941). The life of this great, sad author, who ultimately took her own life, was—as all of her works imply—marked by darkness and light, by desperation and hope, by a profound love of human beings and the knowledge of their loneliness. Her melancholia was her beauty. Her characters were quarrelsome. Wandering between dream and reality. This gaze on the world has much in common with the paintings of the artist Miwa Ogasawara, who was raised in Japan and lives in Hamburg. The search for the most profound human foundations drives this artist. In the knowledge that existence is marked by the constant mode of change. Nothing remains the same. There is no "I am so," only a "this is what I am at this moment," "I could be that." We are as mutable as the tides, as the sky, as the light. Motifs that play a key role in the painter's work. Ogasawara reads moments. "Sometimes I think heaven must be one continuous reading," wrote Woolf about her observations. A sentence that also applies to the pictures discussed here.

VOM VERSUCH ZU SEHEN. DER MENSCH IM BILD.

DER BESONDERE BLICK

Es ist dieser verhangene Blick, der das Auge des Betrachters bannt. Ein Blick tiefer Schwere, der sich im Nichts zu verlieren scheint. Müde oder auch erschöpft scheint diese Frau. Vom Leben ermattet. Aber wach. All das gesehen zu haben, was Leben heißt, erschöpft nun Mal. Es ist natürlich kein Zufall, dass Miwa Ogasawara der englischen Schriftstellerin Virginia Woolf (1882–1941) einige Porträts widmet. Das Leben dieser großen, traurigen Schreibenden, die am Ende freiwillig aus dem Leben schied, war – wie es all ihre Texte bedeuten – geprägt von Finsternis und Helligkeit, von Verzweiflung und Hoffnung, von der tiefen Liebe zum Menschen und dem Wissen um dessen Einsamkeit. Ihre Schwermut war ihre Anmut. Ihre Figuren Hadernde. Wandelnd zwischen Traum und Realität. Dieser Blick auf die Welt hat vieles gemein mit den Bildern der in Hamburg lebenden, in Japan aufgewachsenen Künstlerin Miwa Ogasawara. Es ist die Suche nach dem zutiefst Menschlichen, was diese Künstlerin antreibt. In dem Wissen, dass die Existenz geprägt ist vom stetigen Modus der Veränderung. Nichts bleibt, wie es ist. Es gibt kein »so bin ich«, nur ein »das bin ich in diesem Moment«, »das könnte ich sein«. Wir sind wandelbar wie die Gezeiten, wie der Himmel, wie das Licht. Motive, die auch eine große Rolle im Werk der Malerin spielen. Ogasawara liest Momente. »Manchmal denke ich, der Himmel besteht aus ununterbrochenem, niemals

見ることの試みについて 描かれた人

ニコラ·グレーフ

特異なまなざし

見る人を惹きつけてやまないのは、この伏し目がちの視線だ。虚空に消えていくような深く重みを帯びたまなざし。この女は倦み、疲れているように見える。人生に打ちひしがれているようだ。でも意識ははっきりしている。人生のすべてを見尽くし、疲れ果てた今。小笠原美環がイギリスの女性作家ヴァージニア·ウルフ(1882–1941)にいくつかの肖像画を捧げているのは、もちろん偶然とはいえない。自ら命を絶ち生涯を閉じた偉大で憂いに満ちたこの女流作家の人生は、そのすべての著述に表されているように、闇と光、絶望と希望、人間への深い愛とその孤独への洞察によって特徴付けられている。彼女の憂愁は、彼女の雅やかさだった。諍いあう登場人物。夢と現実の間を彷徨う人たち。この世界観は、日本で育ちハンブルクに住む美術作家、小笠原美環の絵画と多くの点で共通している。この美術家を駆り立てるのは、もっとも深い人間性への追求である。存在が絶え間ない変化のモードであることを確信しつつ。変わらないものは何もない。「私はこうだ」はなくて、ただ「今この時、私はこうだ」、「私はこうかもしれない」があるだけだ。この画家の作品でも大きな役割を果たすモチーフ、潮の満ち引きのように、空のように、光のように、私たちは変化する。小笠原は瞬間を読む。ウルフは自分の観察について「時には空が、絶え間なく決して飽きることなく読むことであるように思う」と書いている。この言葉はここでテーマとされる絵画にも当てはまるものだ。

ある人間を読むということは、自分が人間であることと同様に複雑である。それぞれが自分自身の経験、記憶、今の状態に影響された独自の解釈をするからだ。だからこの人を読むということには始めも終わりもない。常に何かしら解明し尽くせないものが

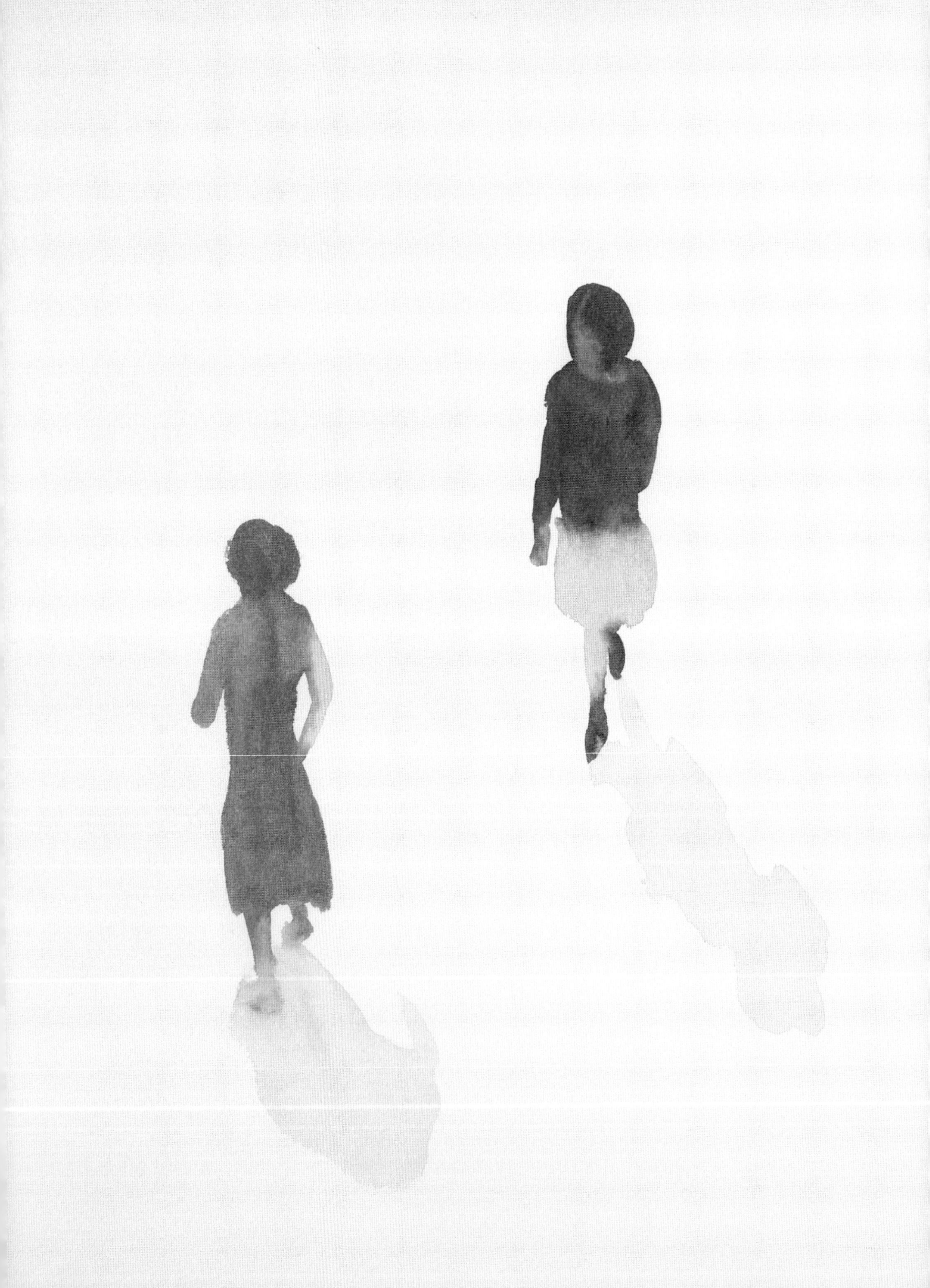

Reading a human is just as complex as being a human. For each reader brings their own interpretation, shaped by their own experiences, own memories, by the situation in which they find themselves at that moment. This reading thus becomes a matter that has neither a beginning nor an end. Something undecipherable always remains, as well as the recognition that it is impossible to grasp the other entirely. Yet we are often concerned with precisely this desire: to be seen and be read, to be understood and protected. We are very fortunate when this occurs. Miwa Ogasawara resolves this dilemma, of wanting to understand a human being's essence, but not being able to, in her own special way. Her painting remains vague, unspecific, implying. There are no details, no clear contours. The artist does not presume to be one who sees completely; she distills out of her observations the essence of being human. Here lies the power of her works. They have a timeless significance.

SOMEHOW.
SOMEWHERE. SOMETIME.

The figures find themselves in undefined spaces. They look out of a window in some direction, they squat on the floor somewhere. They all have in common, however, a (stable) grounding, they are not lost people. The faces are often turned away, show no recognizable feelings. No one laughs. But no one cries either. When several people are visible, then each one is alone, unconnected. Are they alone? Do they feel lonely? This remains unanswered. A great silence is gently revealed in these pictures that reflects the observer back to themselves. What do I recognize, where do I reflect myself, how do I live? Miwa Ogasawara is clever enough to not offer any solutions, no exclusive indications. Perhaps because the painter treats her figures with such tenderness, emphatic and protective. There is no pathos here, no dramatic gestures. It is the careful attempt to quietly get closer to human beings in all of their nuances.

ermüdendem Lesen«, schreibt Woolf über ihre Beobachtungen. Ein Satz, der auch zu den Bildern passt, um die es hier geht.

Einen Menschen zu lesen, ist so komplex, wie selbst Mensch zu sein. Denn jeder Lesende bringt seine Interpretation mit, geprägt von eigenen Erfahrungen, eigenen Erinnerungen, der Situation, in der er sich gerade befindet. So wird dieses Lesen zu einer Angelegenheit, die kein Anfang und kein Ende kennt. Es bleibt immer etwas Unentschlüsselbares zurück und die Erkenntnis, dass es unmöglich ist, ein Gegenüber in Gänze zu erfassen. Und doch geht es uns oft um genau diese Sehnsucht: gesehen und gelesen zu werden, sich verstanden und aufgehoben fühlen. Es ist ein großes Glück, wenn dies passiert. Miwa Ogasawara löst dieses Dilemma, das Wesen des Menschen erfassen zu wollen und es doch nicht können, auf ihre ganz spezifische Weise. Ihre Malerei bleibt im Vagen, im Ungefähren, in der Andeutung. Es gibt keine Details, keine klaren Konturen. Die Künstlerin maßt sich nicht an, vollständig Sehende zu sein, sie destilliert aus ihren Beobachtungen die Essenz des Menschseins. Darin liegt die Kraft ihrer Werke. Sie haben eine zeitlose Gültigkeit.

IRGENDWIE.
IRGENDWO. IRGENDWANN.

Die Figuren befinden sich in unbestimmbaren Räumen. Sie blicken aus einem Fenster ins Irgendwohin, sie hocken auf dem Boden im Irgendwo. Sie alle eint jedoch eine (Boden-) Haftung, sie sind also keine Verlorene. Die Gesichter haben oft eine eigentümliche Abgewandtheit, zeigen keine erkennbaren Gefühle. Da lacht niemand. Da weint aber auch niemand. Und wenn mehrere Menschen zu sehen sind, dann ist dennoch jeder für sich, ungebunden. Sie sind allein? Fühlen sie sich einsam? Das bleibt offen. In den Bildern offenbart sich auf sanfte Weise eine große Schweigsamkeit, die den Betrachter auf sich selbst zurückwirft. Was erkenne ich, wo spiegle ich mich, wie lebe ich? Miwa Ogasawara ist klug genug, uns

あり、向き合う相手の全体を捉えることができないという認識が残る。でも私たちはちょうどそれを望んでいる。見られたい、読まれたい、理解されたい、受け入れられていると感じたいのだ。そうなった時の幸せは大きい。小笠原美環は人間の本質を把握したくてもそれができないというこのジレンマを、彼女に特有の方法で解消している。その絵画は曖昧で漠然とし、暗示的である。細部の描写はなく、明確な輪郭もない。作家はすべてを把握しようと敢えてせずに、観察によって人間性のエッセンスを抽出する。彼女の作品の強みはそこにある。それらの絵画には時代を超えて通じるものがある。

何となく、どこかで、いつか

人物は不確定な空間に描かれている。窓からどこかを見つめていたり、どこかで床にしゃがんでいたりだ。彼らにみな共通しているのは、地に足が着き、自分を見失っていないことだ。彼らは視線を独特に逸らしているので、そこに感情を見てとることができない。誰も笑っていない。でも泣いてもいない。数人が描かれていてもそこには繋がりはなく、それぞれがひとりずつでいる。彼らは孤独なのだろうか。寂しい気持ちでいるのだろうか。その答えはない。絵の中に大きな静寂が優しく現れ、見る人を自分自身へと投げ返す。私は何を認識し、どこに自分を反映させ、どのように生きているのだろう。小笠原美環は賢いことに、私たちにその解答も特別のヒントも与えていない。これらの人物は抽象的なニュアンスにもかかわらず、信じられないほど親密で、捉えどころなく個人的だ。それはおそらく、作家がそれらの人物を愛情を持ち、共感し、保護しながら扱っているからだろう。そこにパトスはなく、大げさな身振りもない。それは人間に、そのすべての陰影の中で静かに接近しようとする慎重な試みだ。

「真実は常に灰色をしている。」
（アンゼルム·キーファー）

小笠原の絵画が無彩色のスペクトルで微妙に変化するのは、偶然ではない。ホワイトグレー、ライトグレー、ミディアムグレー、ダークグレー、ブラックグレー。私たちに意味を訴える色、意味を主張する色はそこにはない。その絵画が問題にしているのは謙虚さである。尊厳である。尊敬の気持ちである。だからこそこの作家の絵画には深遠な人間性がある。

TRUTH IS ALWAYS GRAY

Anselm Kiefer

Ogasawara's painting consequently flickers not by chance in the color spectrum of non-colors: gray-white, light gray, mid-gray, dark gray, black gray. There is no color that imposes meaning, no color that demands meaning. Her paintings are concerned with restraint. With dignity. With respect. This makes the artist's painting profoundly humanistic.

What perhaps is not apparent at first glance is that these pictures are also committed social pictures. They are an attack on all those who believe they have the right answer for everything, who purport to know who they are, how we should live, how the world functions. These paintings are the opposite. They ask questions. They open up the gaze. As vague as her paintings might appear, the artist is uncompromising precisely in this point. She is concerned with gradations. The human between light and shadow, love and desperation, nearness and distance, calmness and anxiety. There is no judgmental brushstroke.

YOUNG LIFE

Again and again we see children. Youth. Girls and boys. In Ogasawara's pictures they do not appear childish but wise. Their faces reveal a perception of the world that is much ahead of us adults. They seem clear in what they see. Their unclouded intuition, their instinct, seems to direct the perception toward the world, to raise questions: Do you not see what is happening? Can you not be more careful? When did you become what you are today? Can you not be more brave, more alive, closer to life—be yourself once again? Less know-it-all? Because you think that it has to be so. Be awake and attentive, curious and unchained. Their gaze is a challenge. We do not conceal our feelings, we are what we are! *Ahnung* (Notion) depicts such a girl. She stands firmly on the ground. Her posture is expectant, in no way fearful. She looks at us and through us. She penetrates us.

keine Lösung anzubieten, keinen exklusiven Hinweis. Diese Figuren sind trotz ihrer abstrakten Nuancen unfassbar nah, unbegreiflich persönlich. Vielleicht liegt es daran, dass die Malerin so liebevoll mit ihren Figuren umgeht, empathisch und beschützend. Da ist kein Pathos, keine große Geste. Es ist der vorsichtige Versuch, sich dem Menschen leise anzunähern in all seinen Schattierungen.

DIE WAHRHEIT
IST IMMER GRAU.

Anselm Kiefer

So changiert Ogasawaras Malerei nicht zufällig im Farbspektrum der Nichtfarben, weißgrau, hellgrau, mittelgrau, dunkelgrau, schwarzgrau. Es gibt keine Farbe, die uns Bedeutung aufdrängt, keine Farbe, die uns Bedeutung zumutet. Es geht in ihren Bildern um Zurückhaltung. Um Würde. Um Respekt. Damit ist die Malerei dieser Künstlerin zutiefst humanistisch.

Was vielleicht auf den ersten Blick nicht so scheinen mag, so sind diese Bilder damit auch engagierte Gesellschaftsbilder. Sie sind ein Angriff gegen all jene, die glauben, auf alles die richtige Antwort zu haben, die vorgeben zu wissen, wer wir sind, wie wir leben sollen, wie die Welt funktioniert. Diese Bilder sind das Gegenteil. Sie stellen Fragen. Sie öffnen den Blick. So vage ihre Bilder erscheinen mögen, in diesem Punkt ist die Künstlerin kompromisslos präzise. Es geht um Zwischentöne. Der Mensch zwischen Licht und Schatten, zwischen Liebe und Verzweiflung, Nähe und Distanz, Ruhe und Unruhe. Es gibt keinen urteilenden Pinselstrich

DAS JUNGE LEBEN

Und immer wieder sehen wir Kinder. Jugendliche. Mädchen und Jungen. In Ogasawaras Bildern erscheinen sie nicht kindlich, eher weise. Ihre Gesichter bezeugen eine Wahrnehmung auf die Welt, die uns Erwachsenen weit voraus ist. Sie wirken klar, in dem, was

最初の一瞥ではそう見えなくても、これらの絵画はそれ故、社会にコミットしている。何についても正しい答えを持っていると信じる人たちがいる。私たちが誰で、どのように生きるべきか、世界がどのように機能するかを知っているふりをする人たちがいる。これらの絵画はそういう人間へ攻撃だ。その正反対だからだ。それらは問いを投げかける。目を覚まさせる。もし小笠原の絵画が茫洋としているように見えても、この点において作家は容赦なく、妥協を許さない。そこでは中間トーンが大切だ。光と影の間、愛と絶望、近·遠、安静と不穏の間に存在する人間。そこに判断を下すような筆使いは見られない。

若い生命

そして繰り返し子供たちが描かれている。若者、少女、少年。小笠原の絵では、彼らは子供っぽいというよりむしろ賢く見える。私たち大人よりも、世界をはるかに先取りして知覚していることが、その顔に現れている。彼らは何を見ているかを確信している。彼らの濁りない直観、その本能は世界に対する知覚にオリエンテーションを与え、問いを投げかける。あなたたちには何が起こっているか見えないの。気を付けることができないの。あなたたちはいつから今みたいになってしまったの。もっと大胆に、生き生きとして、もっと人生そのものを生きて—もっと自分らしくなれないの。知ったかぶりはもうやめて。こうであるべきと信じているからだ。目を覚まし注意深く、興味を持ち、束縛を解いて。彼女たちの目つきは挑戦的だ。私たちは気持ちを隠したりしない、私たちはあるがまま。*Ahnung*（予感）にはそんな少女が描かれている。少女はしっかりと立っている。何かを待っているような佇まい、不安な様子はみじんもない。この少女は私たちを見つめ、すっかり洞察している。見抜いている。

「光が明るく見えるには、
闇もなくてはならない。」

（フランシス·ベーコン）

小笠原の絵は私たちを置き去りにしない。これらの絵画は対話を求めている。ここでも深く人間的だ。それらは私たちに繰り返し希望を与える。そこには光があり、海遊びがあり、踊る人がいる。ここでも大事なのは常に憧れだ。親愛と思いやり。ひとりぼっちの、カップルの、自分を見失った、懐疑的な、または確信を求める、そのような人間の存在への深い理解。そこで

IN ORDER FOR THE LIGHT
TO SHINE SO BRIGHTLY,
THE DARKNESS MUST BE PRESENT

Francis Bacon

Ogasawara's paintings do not leave us untouched. These pictures seek a dialogue. Here too they are profoundly human. They continually provide us with hope. There is light there, playing in the sea, dancers. The pictures are always concerned with yearning. Affection and devotion. A profound understanding of the human as a being that is lonely, alone in a pair, lost, skeptical, or seeking certainties. These pictures are always about possibilities. About potential change, mistrust against stagnancy. If one spun her motifs further, then everything could change in the next moment. The sitting girl would stand up, the young woman looking out the window would turn again to the room, the group of people at the sea would move on to the beach after swimming. There is always the option of a new perspective; it is actually conceived in the picture. Light and shadow. No moment remains as it was. That is the great opportunity of being human. I can always rethink myself: I am flexible. I is I is I is I.

ONE IS NOT BORN, BUT
RATHER BECOMES, A WOMAN

Simone de Beauvoir

Then there are the women who wanted movement, who dared it. Who knew who they wanted to be, how they wanted to change the world. These are almost the only paintings with initials, with indications. They mean a lot to the painter. Women who directed all of their energy into self-determination and freedom. *V. W.* (Virginia Woolf), *Rosa* (Rosa Luxemburg), *Simone* (Simone de Beauvoir). Women who fought and did not let themselves be irritated or intimidated by male dominance. Who lived out their ideas. Who questioned role models and themselves became role models. "For me an idea is not theoretical, one experiences it; *sie sehen. Ihre ungetrübte Intuition, ihr Instinkt scheinen die Wahrnehmung auf die Welt zu lenken, werfen Fragen auf: Seht ihr nicht, was passiert? Könnt ihr nicht aufpassen? Wann seid ihr so geworden, wie ihr heute seid? Könnt ihr nicht wagemutiger, lebendiger, näher am Leben dran sein – wieder mehr ihr selbst sein? Weniger besserwisserisch. Weil ihr denkt, so müsste es sein. Seid wach und aufmerksam, neugierig und entfesselbar. Ihr Blick wirkt wie eine Aufforderung. Wir verheimlichen keine Gefühle, wir sind, wie wir sind! Ahnung zeigt so ein Mädchen. Es steht fest auf dem Boden. Die Körperhaltung abwartend, keineswegs ängstlich. Es schaut uns an und durch uns durch. Es durchschaut uns.*

DAMIT DAS LICHT SO HELL
SCHEINEN KANN, MUSS
ES AUCH DUNKELHEIT GEBEN.

Francis Bacon

Ogasawaras Bilder lassen uns nicht zurück. Diese Bilder suchen den Dialog. Auch hier sind sie zutiefst menschlich. Sie geben uns immer wieder Hoffnung. Da ist Licht, das Spiel im Meer, Tanzende. Hier geht es auch immer um Sehnsucht. Zuneigung und Hinwendung. Ein tiefes Verständnis für den Menschen als einsames, zweisames, verlorenes, zweiflerisches oder nach Gewissheit suchendes Wesen. Es geht immer um Möglichkeiten. Um potenzielle Veränderung, dem Misstrauen gegen Stillstand. Würde man ihre Motive weiterdenken, dann könnte sich im nächsten Moment wieder alles verändern. Das Mädchen, das sitzt, würde aufstehen, die aus dem Fenster blickende junge Frau würde sich wieder dem Raum zuwenden, die Gruppe im Meer würde sich nach dem Bad zum Strand bewegen. Es gibt also immer die Option auf eine neue Perspektive, sie wird geradezu mitgedacht. Licht und Schatten. Kein Moment bleibt, wie er ist. Das ist die große Chance am Mensch sein. Ich kann mich immer neu denken, ich bin beweglich. Ich ist ich ist ich ist ich.

は常に可能性が、可能な変化が重要だ。静止状態への不信感。描かれたモティーフについて想定するならば、次の瞬間にはすべてが変化するだろう。座っている少女は立ち上がり、窓辺の若い女は再び部屋の方を向くだろう。海のグループは泳いだ後で砂浜に向かうだろう。常に新しいパースペクティブのためのオプションがあり、それは初めから考慮されているようだ。光と影。どんな瞬間もそのままに留まることはない。これは人間であることの大きなチャンスだ。私はいつでも新しく自分を考えることができ、流動的だ。私は私で私であり私である。

「人は女に生まれるわけではない、
女になるのだ」

（シモーヌ·ドゥ·ボーヴォワール）

そして、そこには動きを求めて挑戦した女たちがいる。自分たちが誰になりたいのか、いかに世界を変えたいのか、彼女たちにはわかっていた。それらはほとんどが単独の作品で、イニシャルとヒントで暗示されている。画家にとって重要な意味を持つ女たち。独立と自由のためにエネルギーのすべてを注いだ女たち。*V. W.*（ヴァージニア·ウルフ）、*Rosa*（ローザ·ルクセンブルク）、*Simone*（シモーヌ·ドゥ·ボーヴォワール）。闘い、男性優位にも怯むことなく、恐れを知らなかった女たち。自分の思想に忠実だった女たち。彼女たちは与えられた役割に疑問を抱き、自ら規範的な存在となった。「ひとつの考えは理論的なものではないわ。人はそれを体験するのよ。もしそれが理論的なものでしかなかったら、何の役にも立たないわ。」これはボーヴォワールの小説『招かれた女』の登場人物フランソワーズの言葉だ。どの時代にも必要とされる女たち。ほかのやり方も可能だ、他の方法を取らなければならないと世界を鼓吹する女たち。無知、凡庸、視野の狭さ、ナルシシズムに逆らいつつ。「アダムは粗野な考案でしかなかった。」（シモーヌ·ドゥ·ボーヴォワール）考案は考案に過ぎない。一つの案には常に反対案もある。

「人は、内心の極限に達しようと
試みなければならない。」

（サミュエル·ベケット）

人は小笠原美環の絵を全身で感じとる。彼女の絵を見ることは、感じることに避けようなく繋がる。広大な画面を目の前にして、見る人はそこに浸ることができる。力を抜いて。霧の中にさまよいこんだみ

if it remains theoretical it is of no use." This is what the character Françoise says in Beauvoir's novel *She Came to Stay.* The women that each era needs. Women who impress upon the world that things can be different, must be different. Against ignorance, banality, narrowmindedness, narcissism. "Adam was only a rough draft" (Simone de Beauvoir). A draft is a draft. For every draft there is also a counterdraft.

ONE MUST TRY TO GO
INSIDE TO THE UTMOST

Samuel Beckett

You feel Miwa Ogasawara's pictures. In her work, seeing inevitably becomes feeling. Since there is so much surface, as an observer one can plunge into it. Let oneself fall into it. As though one wandered into a fog. Everything becomes blurry. You walk a bit further, try to orient yourself, and ultimately the picture gets clearer. Recognition arrives only with time, with the readiness to engage, to move in the picture. For this reason her paintings get so close to you. There is a lot of space there for us. We are figures in a picture. How comforting.

MAN KOMMT NICHT ALS FRAU ZUR
WELT, MAN WIRD DAZU GEMACHT.

Simone de Beauvoir

Und dann sind da die Frauen, die Bewegung wollten, sie herausforderten. Die wussten, wer sie sein wollten, wie sie die Welt verändern wollten. Es sind die nahezu einzigen Bilder, mit Initialen, mit Hinweisen. Sie bedeuten der Malerin viel. Frauen, die all ihre Energie in ihre Selbstbestimmung und Freiheit legten. V.W. *(Virginia Woolf),* Rosa *(Rosa Luxemburg),* Simone *(Simone de Beauvoir). Frauen, die kämpften und sich von der Dominanz der Männer nicht irritieren oder einschüchtern ließen. Die ihre Ideen lebten. Die Rollenbilder infrage stellten und selbst zum Rolemodel wurden. »Für mich ist eine Idee nichts Theoretisches, man erlebt sie; wenn sie theoretisch bleibt, taugt sie nichts.« Das sagt die Figur Françoise in Beauvoirs Roman* Sie kam und sie blieb. *Frauen, wie jede Zeit sie braucht. Frauen, die der Welt einschärfen, dass es auch anders geht, anders gehen muss. Gegen Ignoranz, Banalität, Engstirnigkeit, Narzissmus. »Adam war nichts als ein roher Entwurf« (Simone de Beauvoir). Ein Entwurf ist ein Entwurf. Zu jedem Entwurf gibt es auch einen Gegenentwurf.*

MAN MUSS VERSUCHEN,
BIS ZUM ÄUSSERSTEN
INS INNERE ZU GEHEN.

Samuel Beckett

Miwa Ogasawaras Bilder fühlt man. Das Sehen wird bei ihr unweigerlich zum Fühlen. Weil so viel Fläche da ist, kann man als Betrachter eintauchen. Sich fallen lassen. Es ist, als ob man in einen Nebel geraten ist. Alles verschwimmt. Dann läuft man vorsichtig weiter, versucht sich zu orientieren, und irgendwann klärt sich das Bild wieder. Das Erkennen kommt erst mit der Zeit, mit der Bereitschaft, sich einzulassen, sich im Bild zu bewegen. Aus diesem Grund sind ihre Bilder so nah an einem dran. Da ist viel Raum für uns. Wir sind Figuren in einem Bild. Wie wohltuend.

たいだ。すべてがぼんやりしている。それでも慎重に歩き、方向を定めようとしているうちに、次第に絵は晴れていく。認識は時間をかけてもたらされる、もし関わり合う意思があれば、その絵の中を動き回る気があれば。小笠原の絵画が私たちにまったく身近なのは、そのためだ。そこには私たちのための空間が溢れるようにある。私たちが絵の中の人物だ。何と心地よいことだろう。

p. 30 *19.14 / 2019*
53×38 cm / Ink on paper

p. 35 *19.09 / 2019*
39×28 cm / Ink on paper

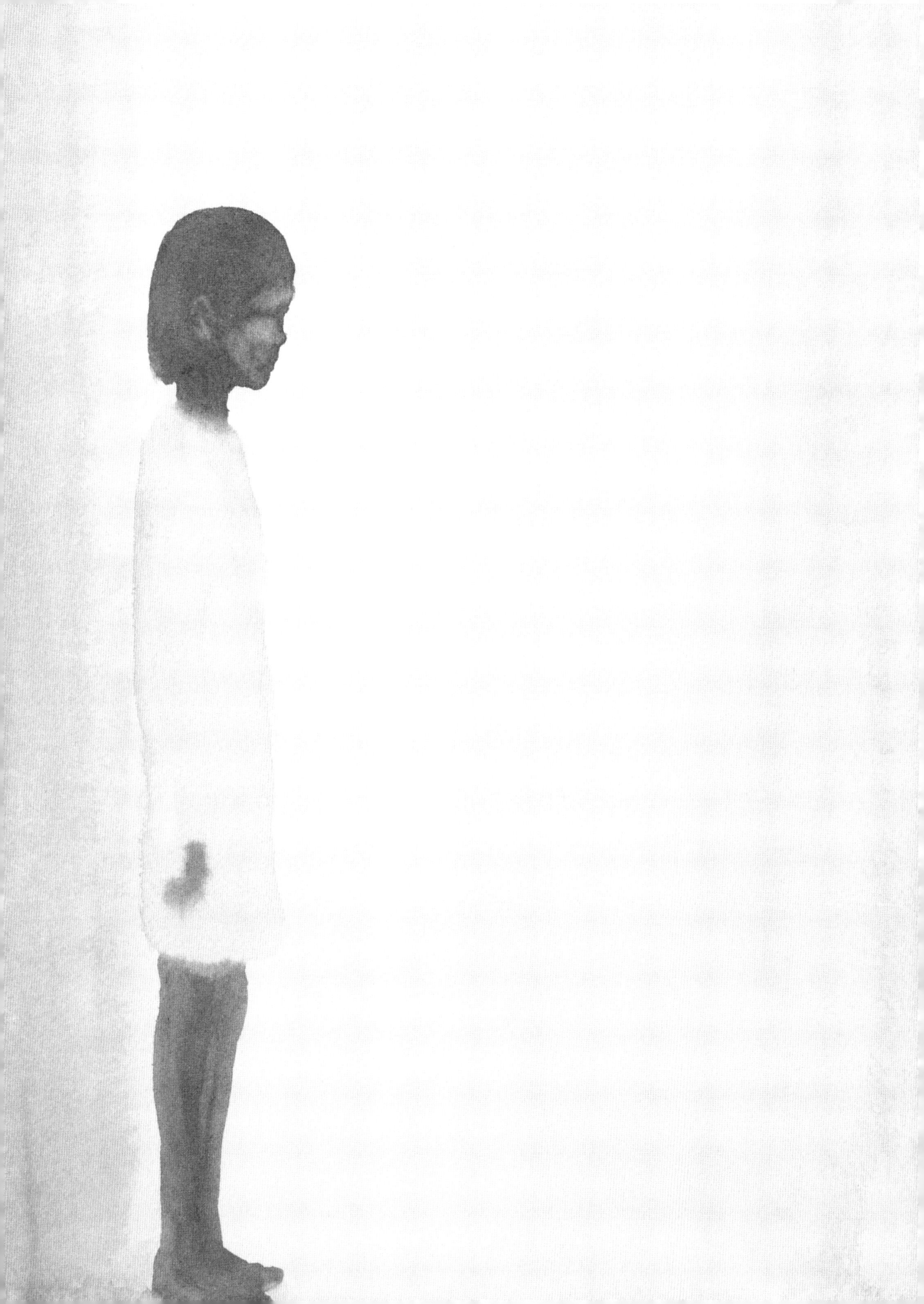

VESSEL 30 2019 / 60 × 50 cm

RAUM 7 2014 / 40 × 35 cm EINSICHT > 2020 / 130 × 180 cm

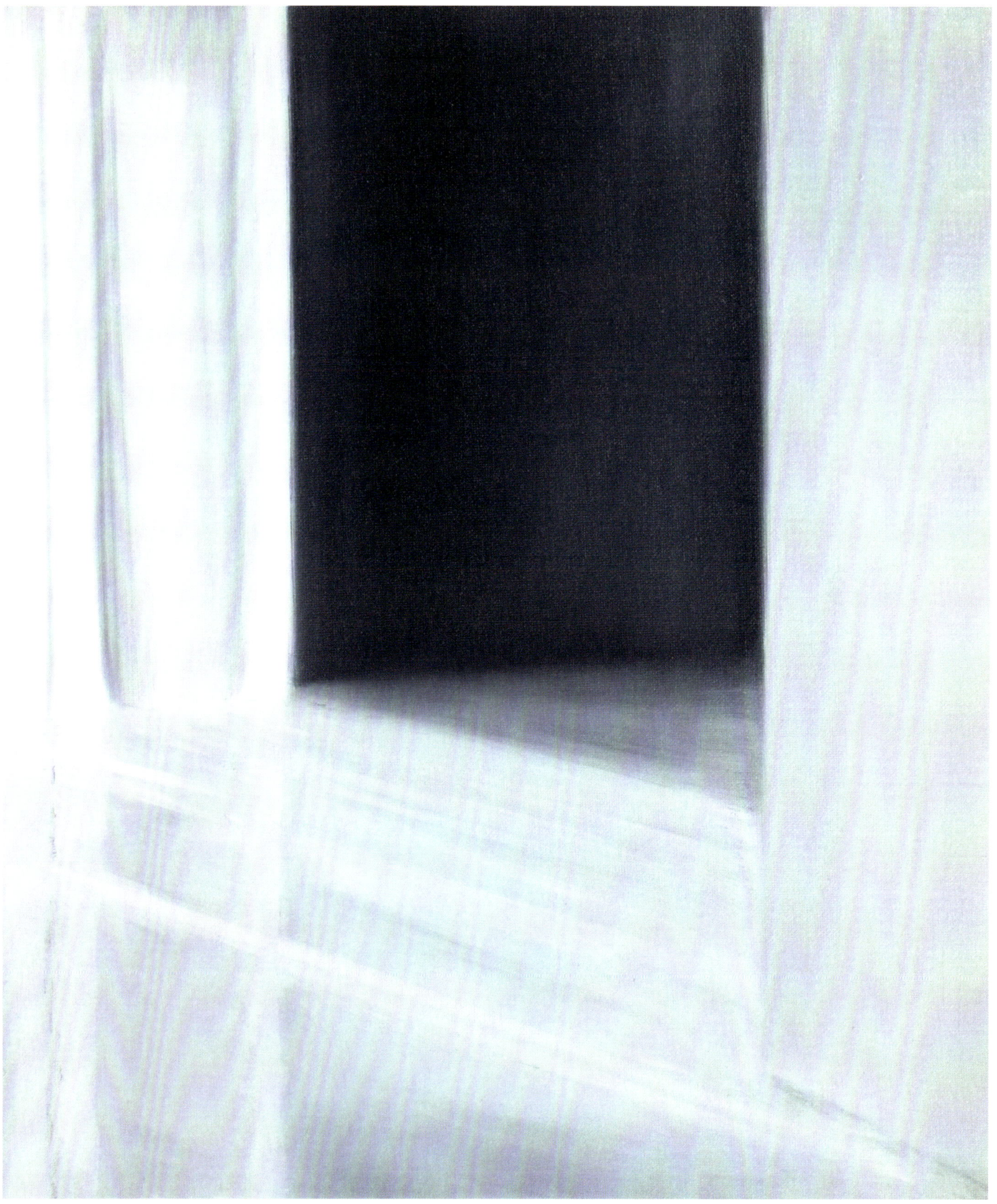

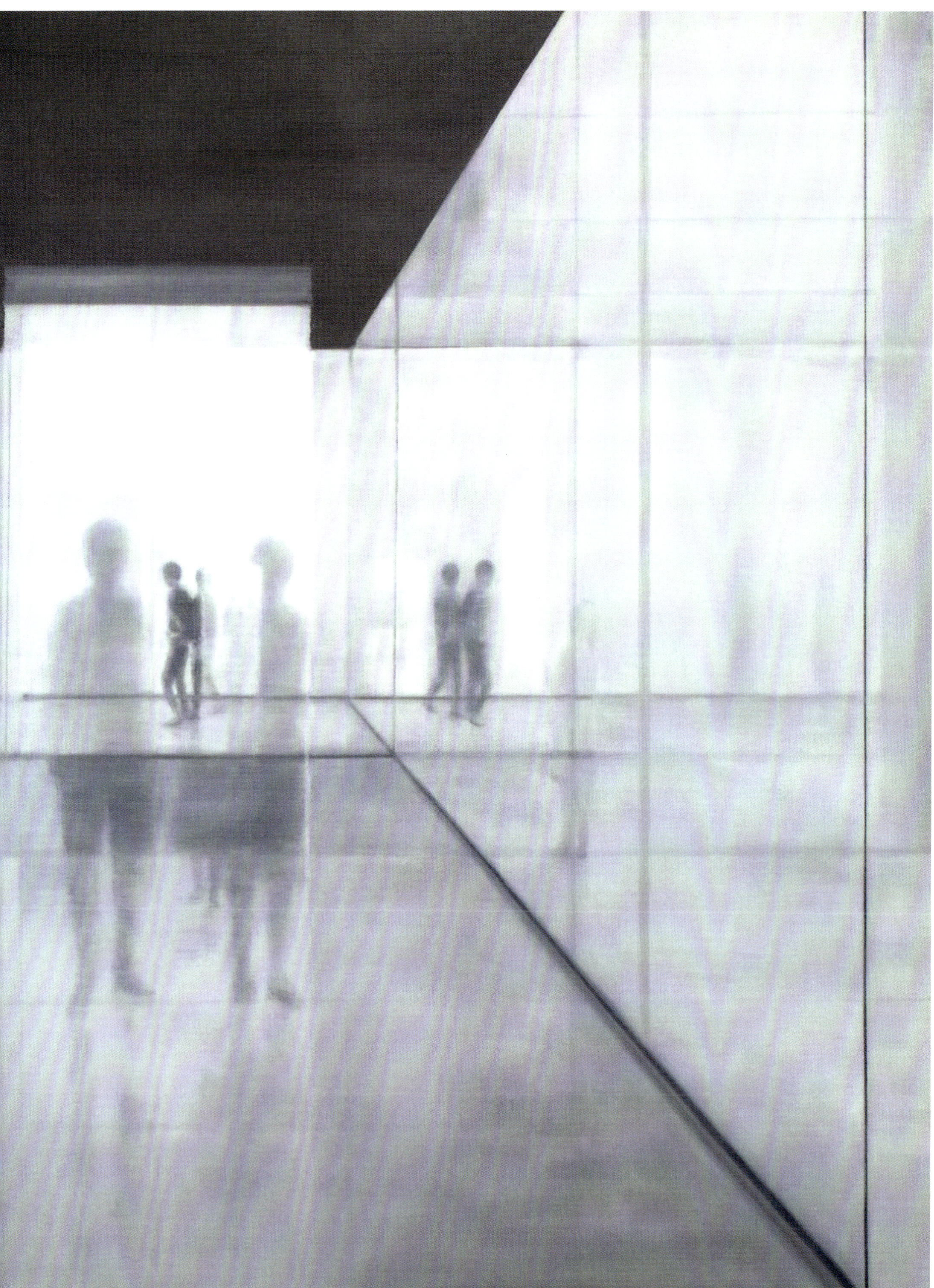

GLASKUGEL 1 2015 / 70 × 50 cm

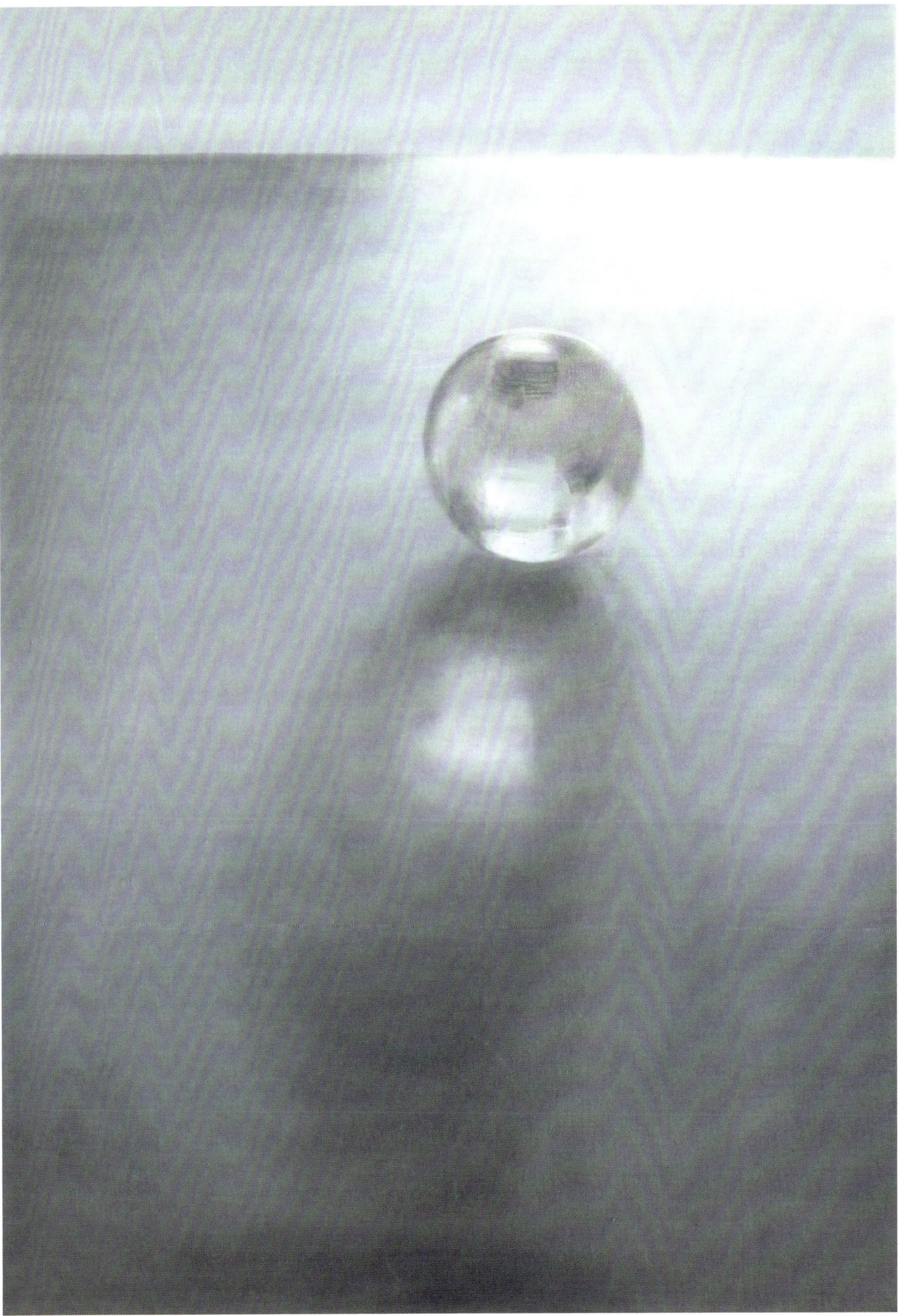

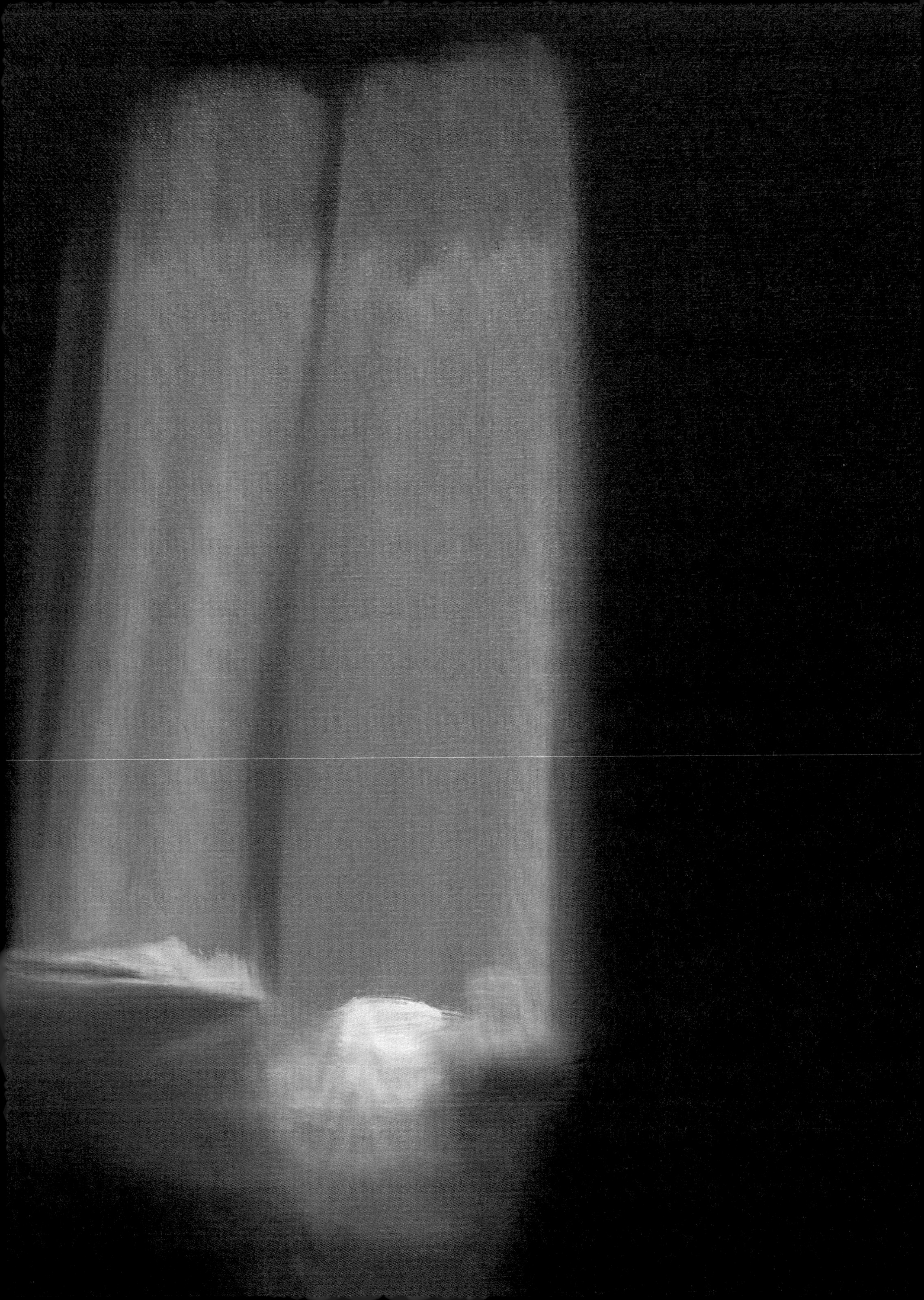

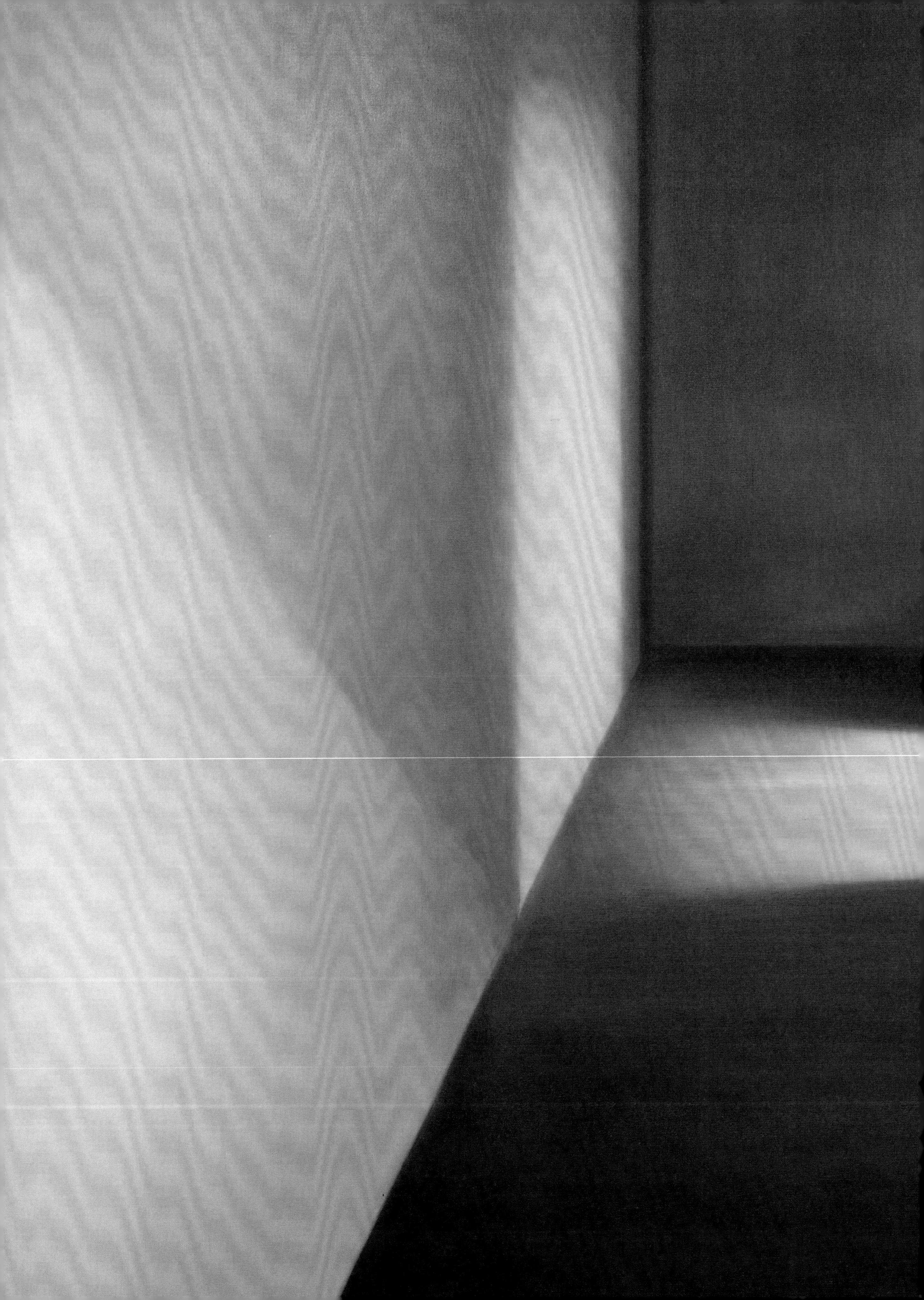

KOWAREMONO 2018 / 50 × 40 cm

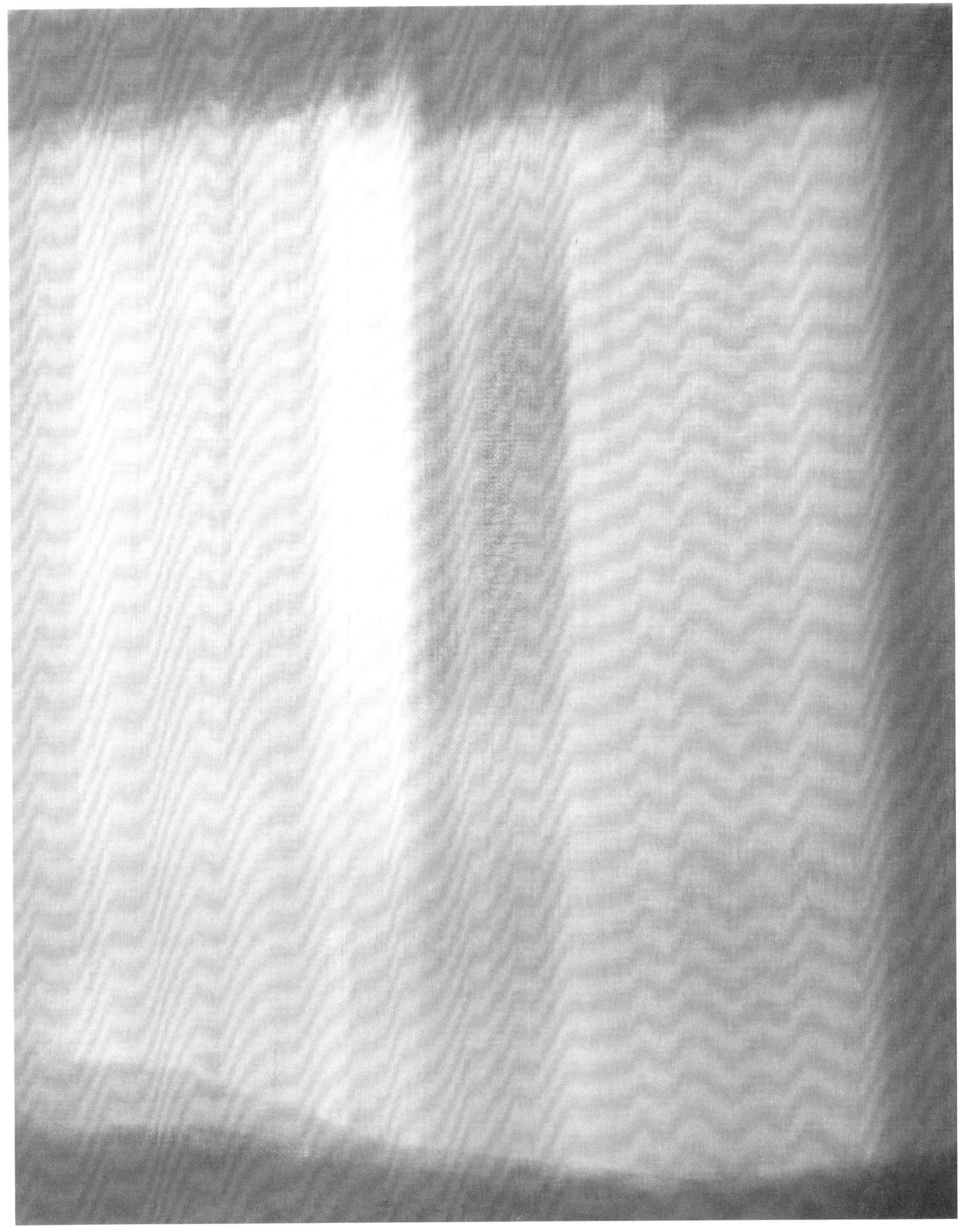

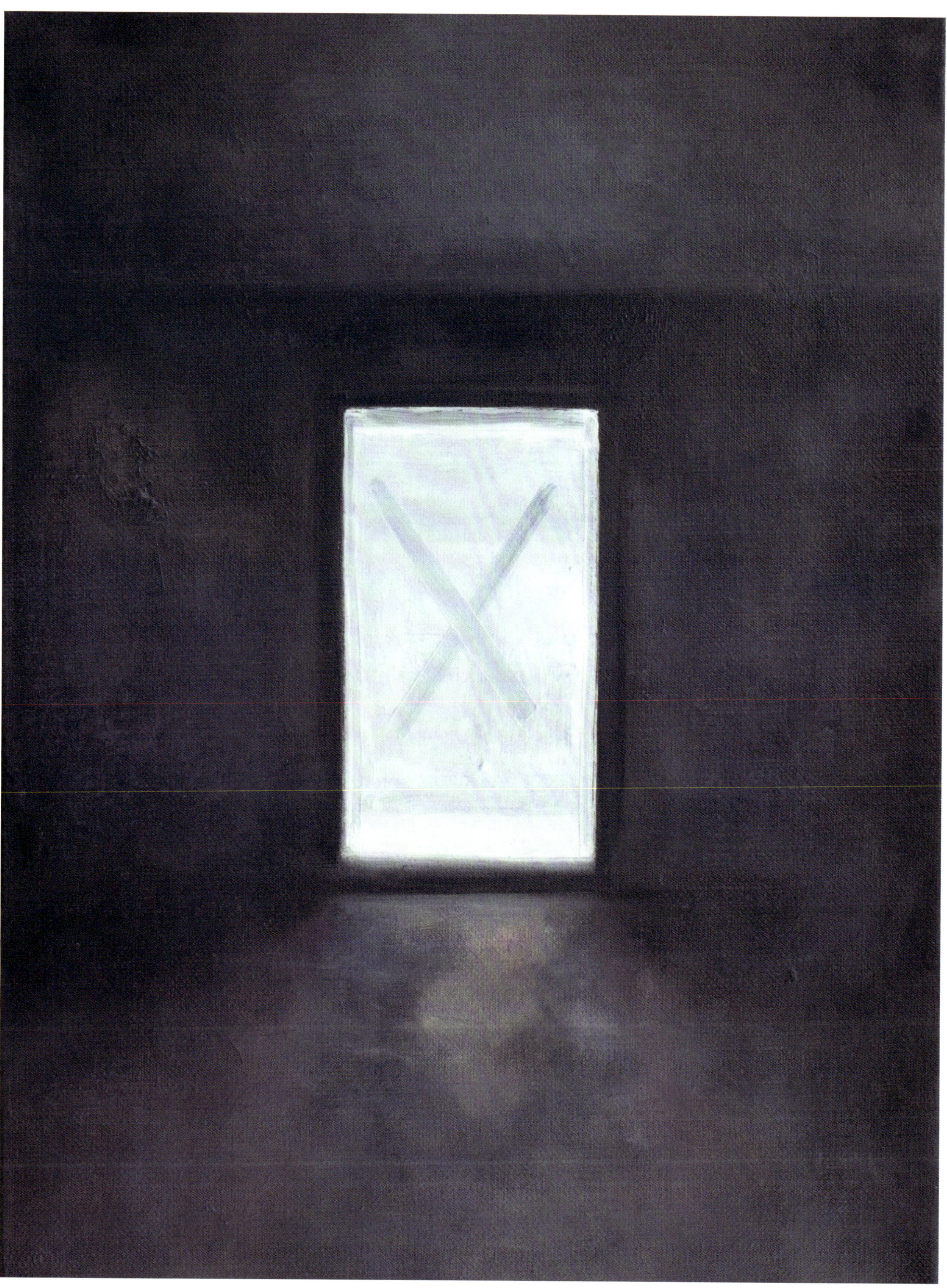

 ZWISCHENRAUM 8 2018 / 40 × 30 cm

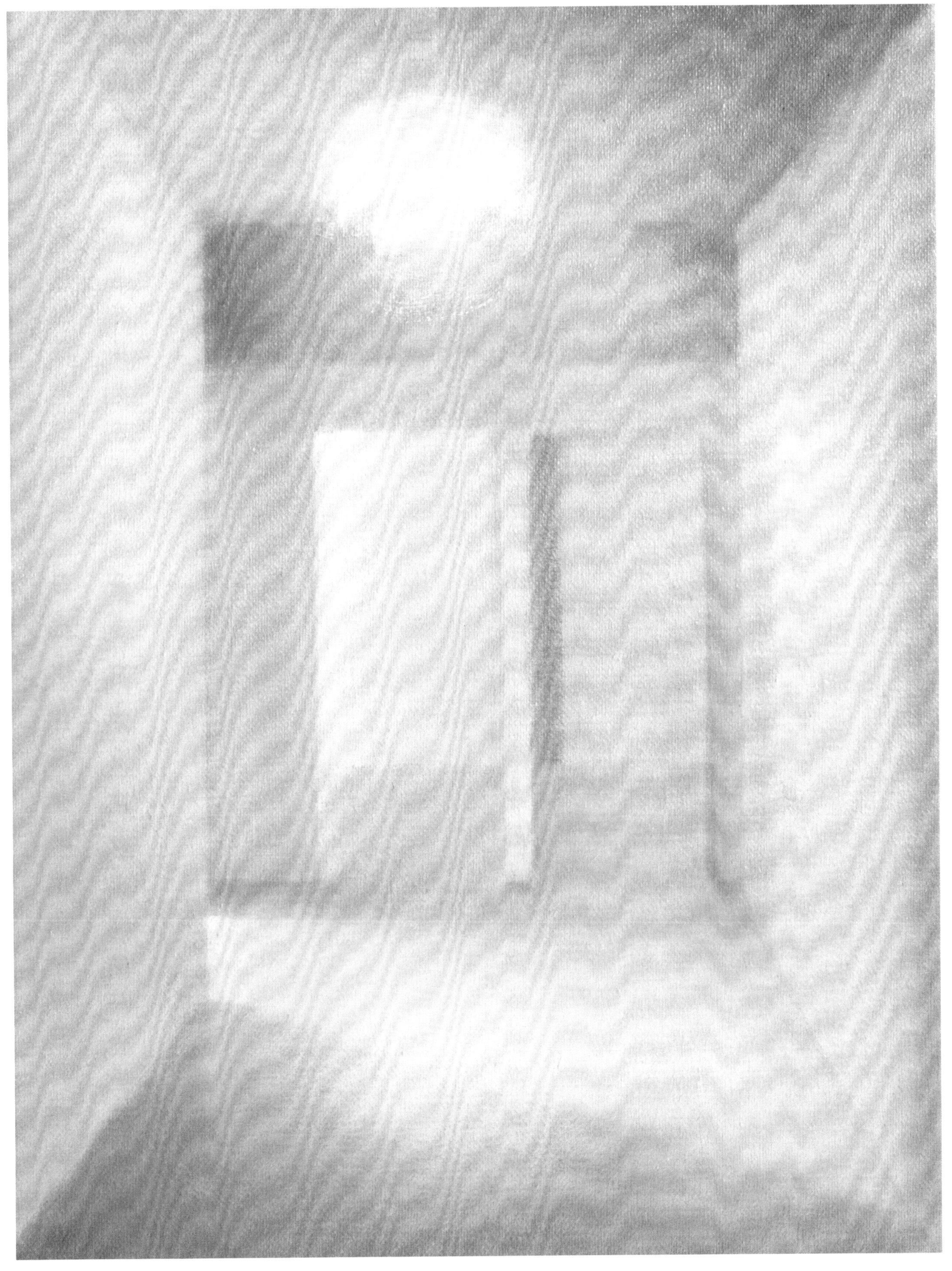

ZWISCHENRAUM 6 2018 / 40 × 30 cm

CURTAIN 2019 / 40 × 40 cm INBETWEEN > 2013 / 150 × 120 cm + 150 × 120 cm

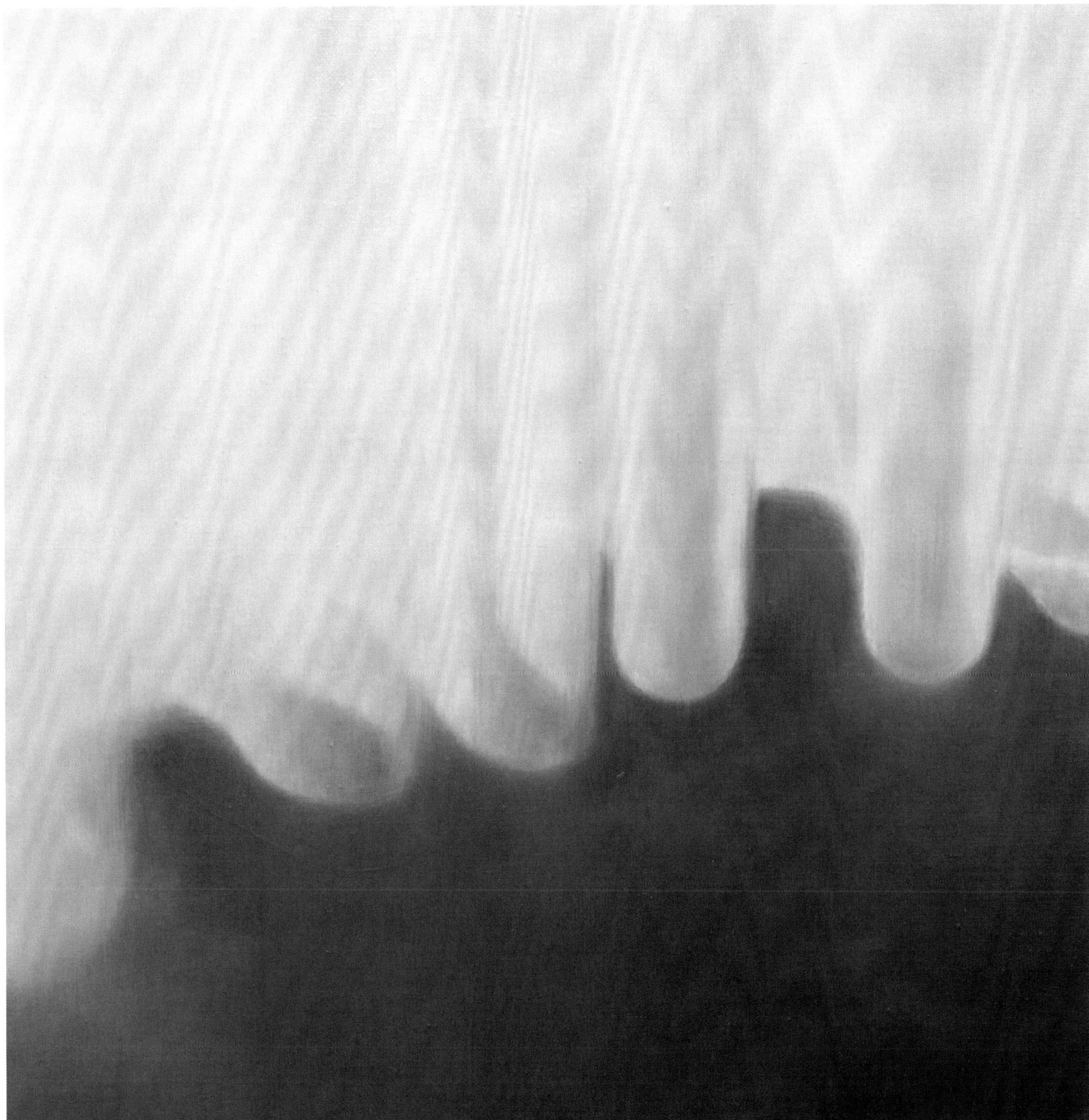

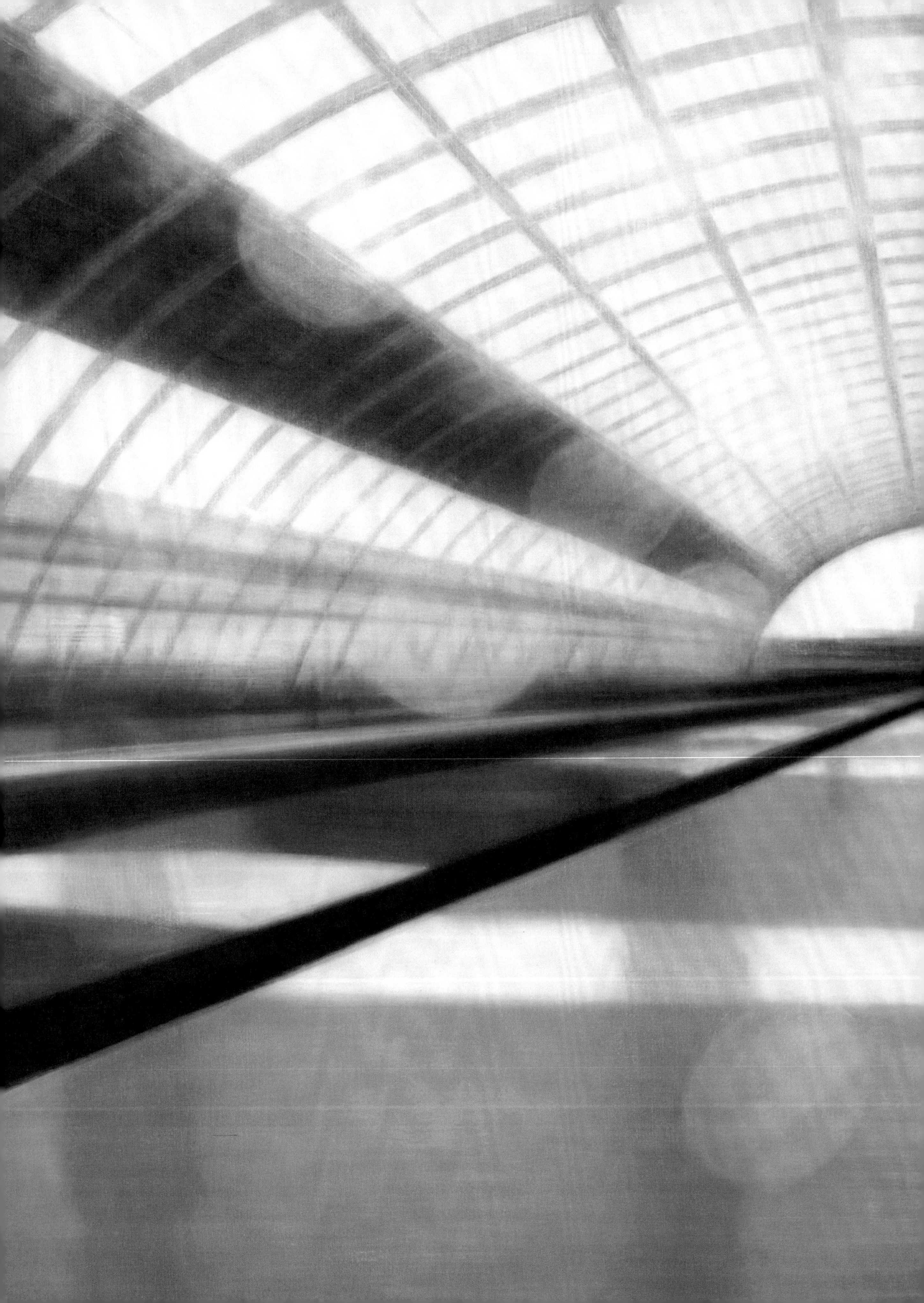

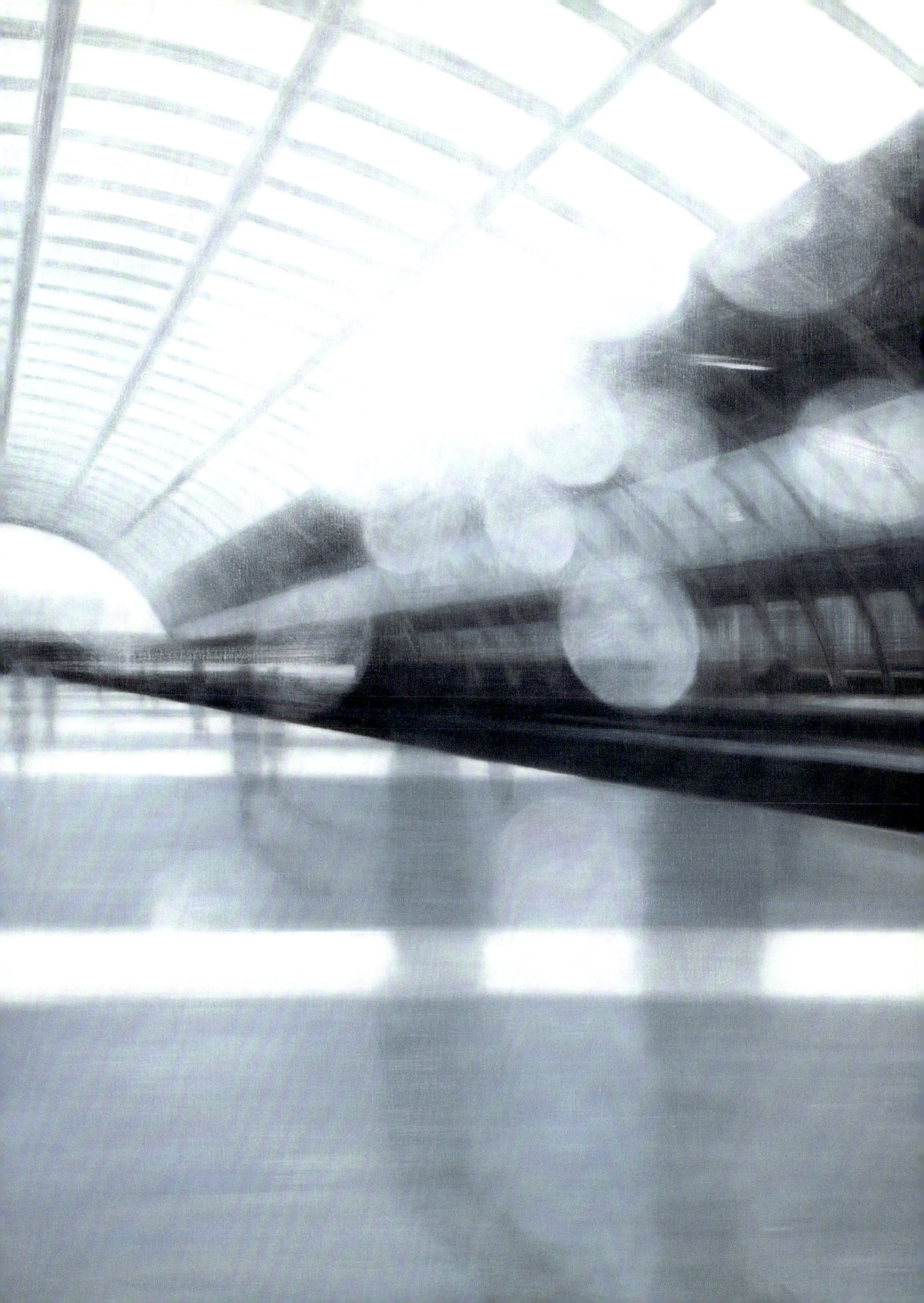

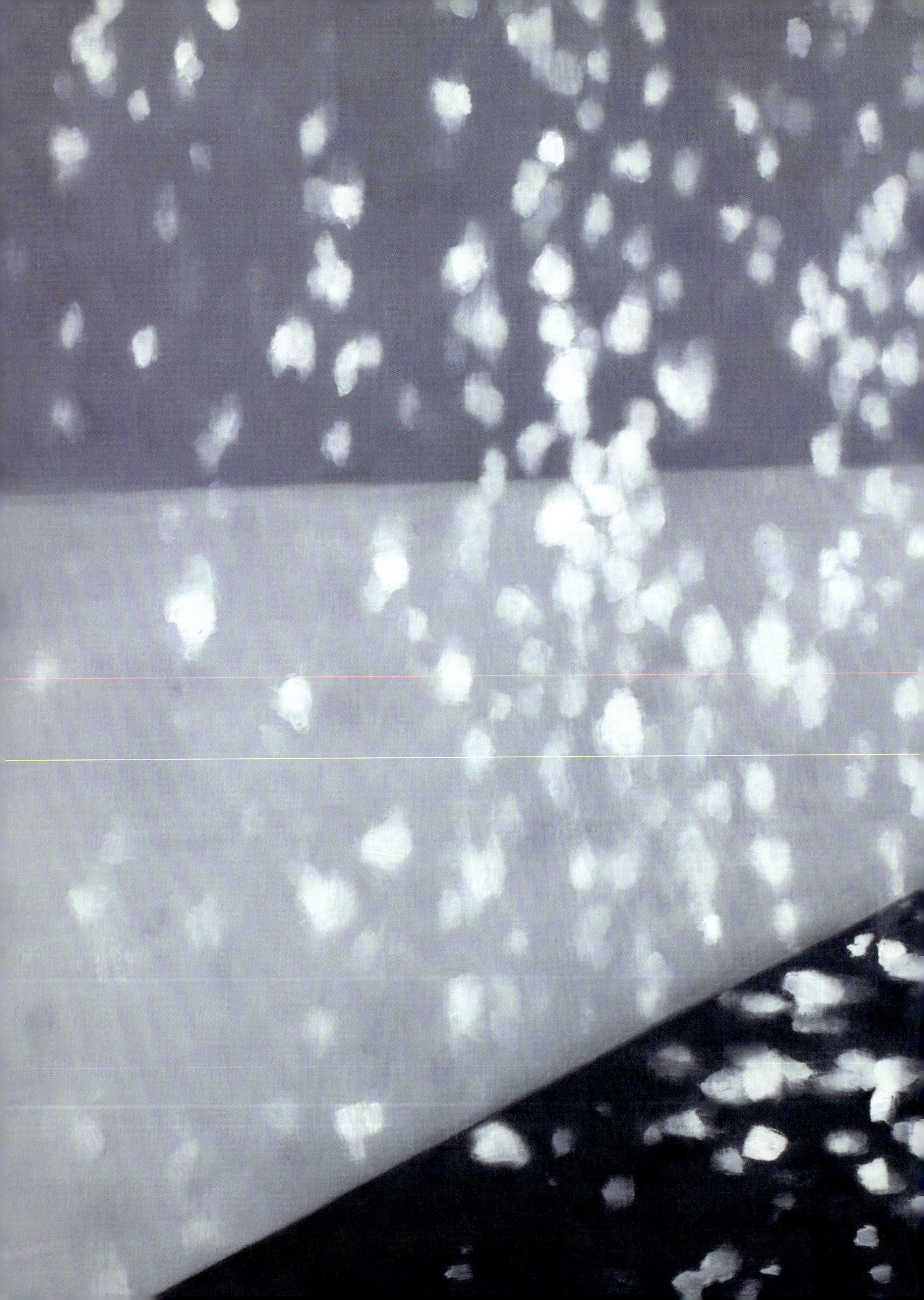

MEMORIES 4 2017 / 100 × 80 cm

GLASKUGEL 5 2019 / 70 × 50 cm

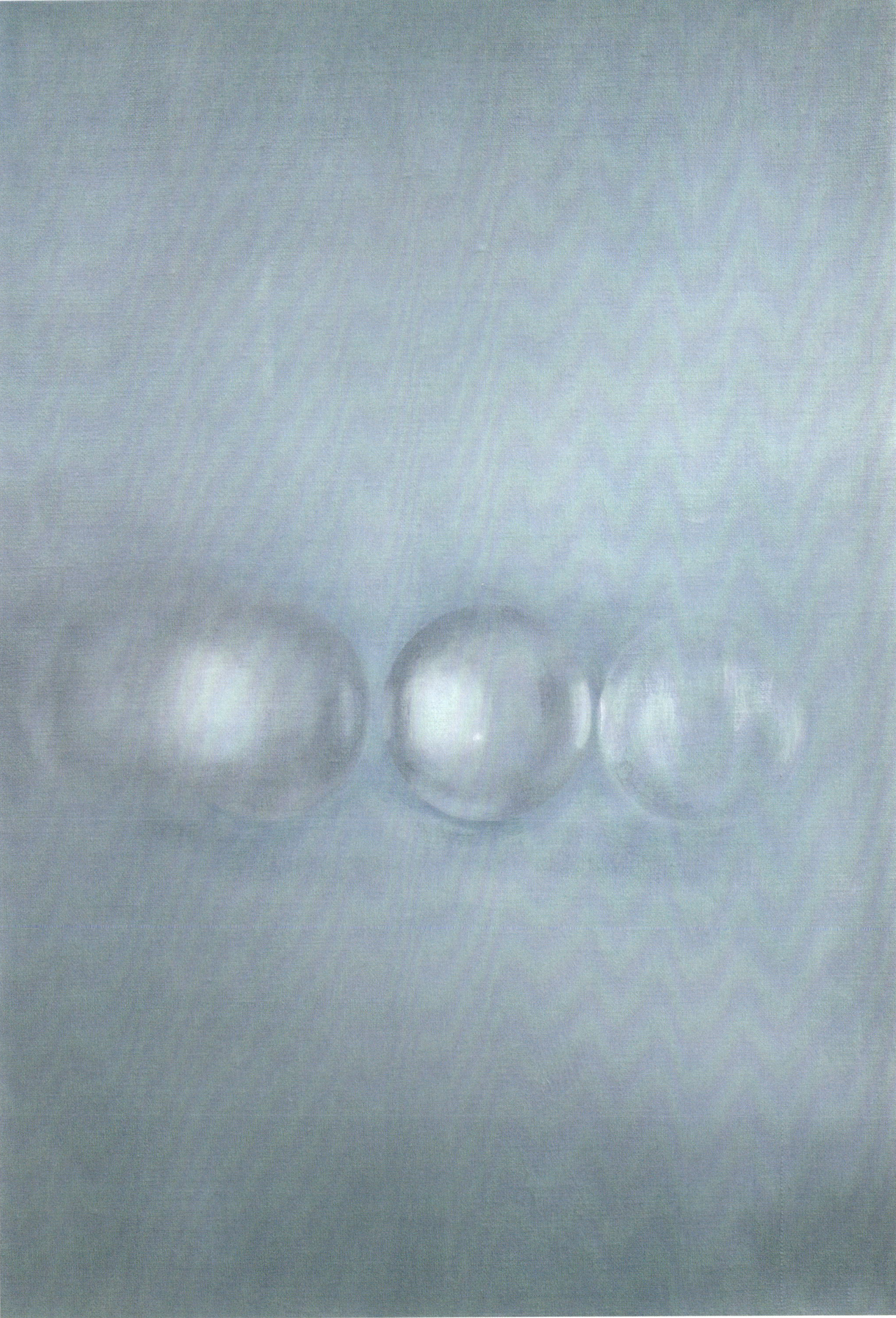

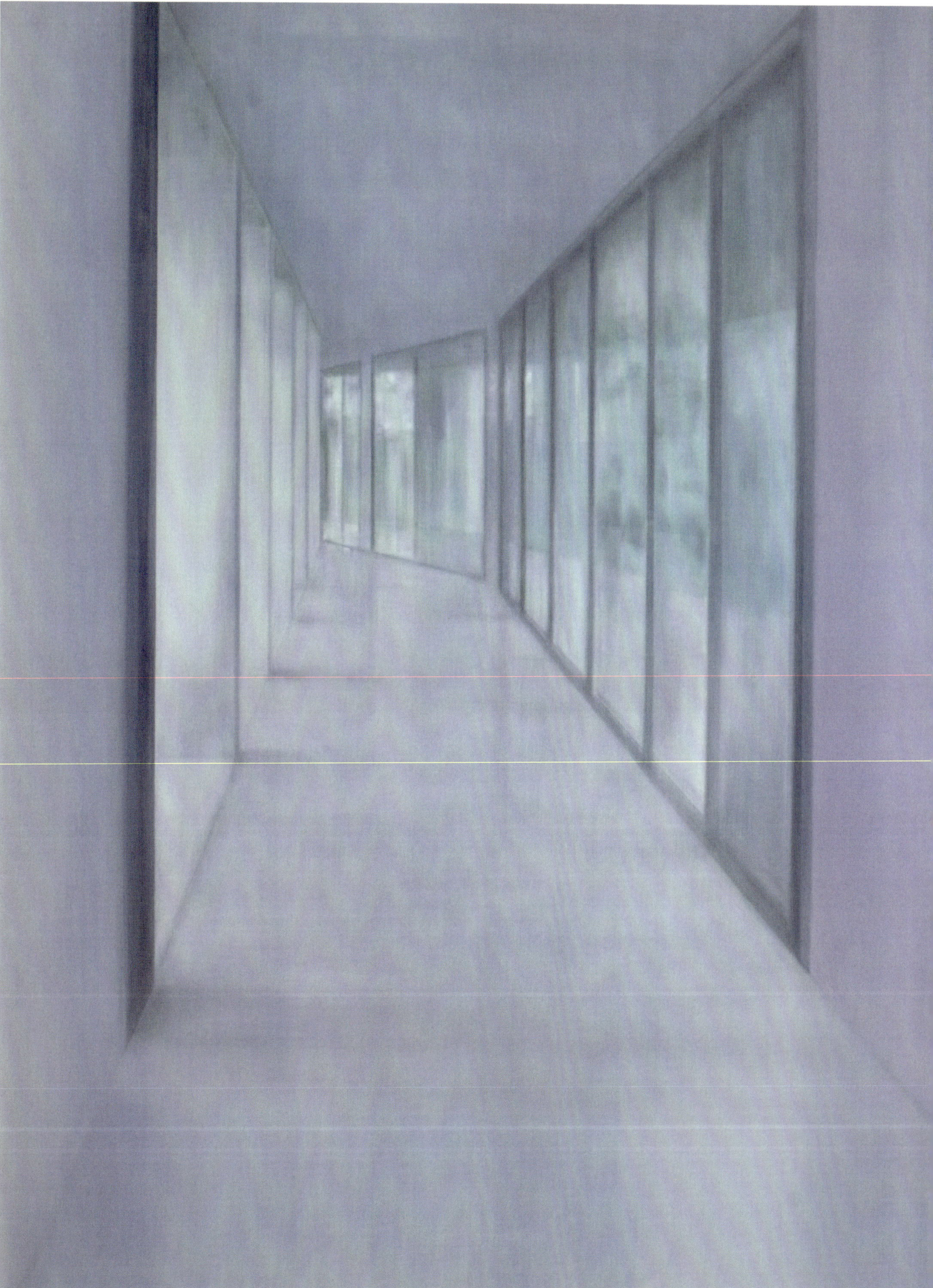

PASSAGE 2016 / 160 × 140 cm

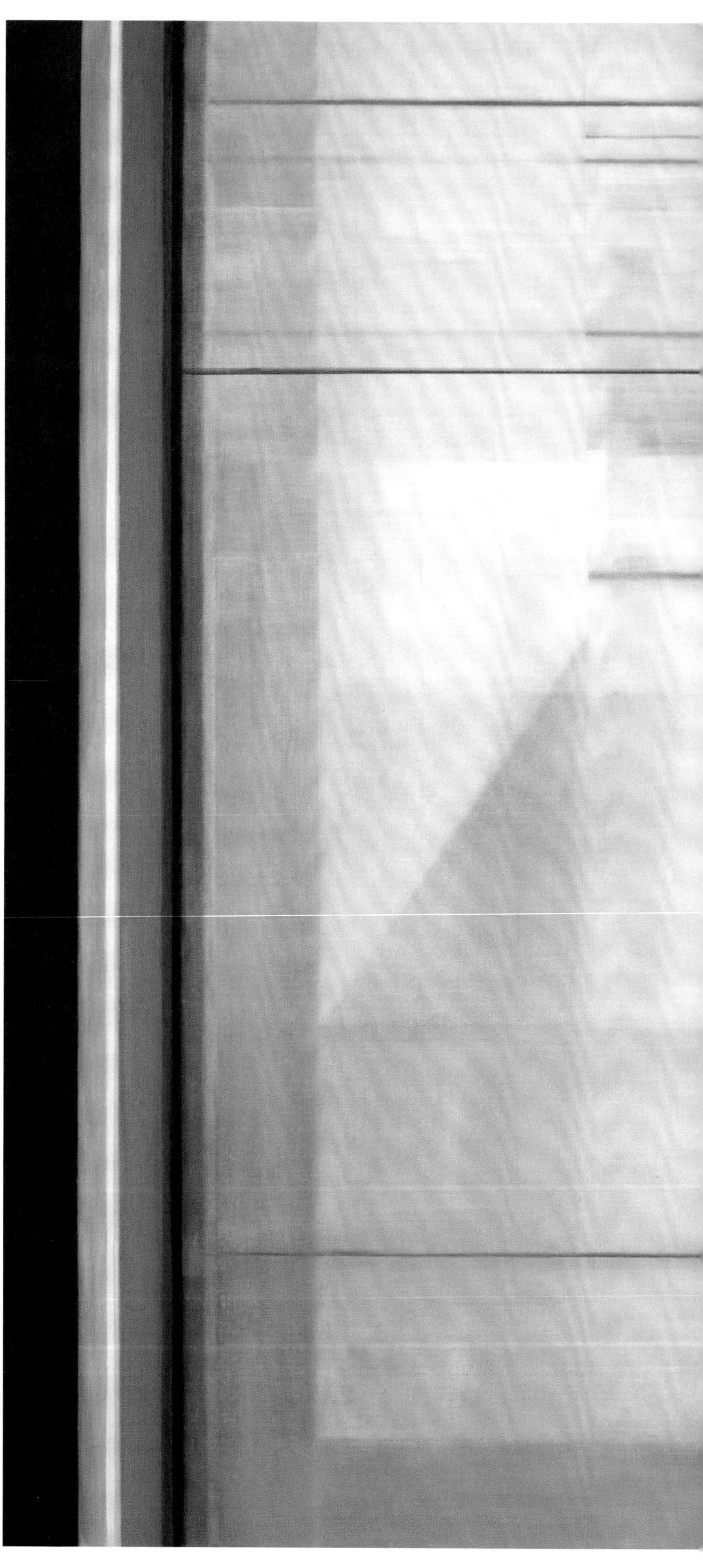

 BLICKWINKEL 2020 / 130 × 170 cm

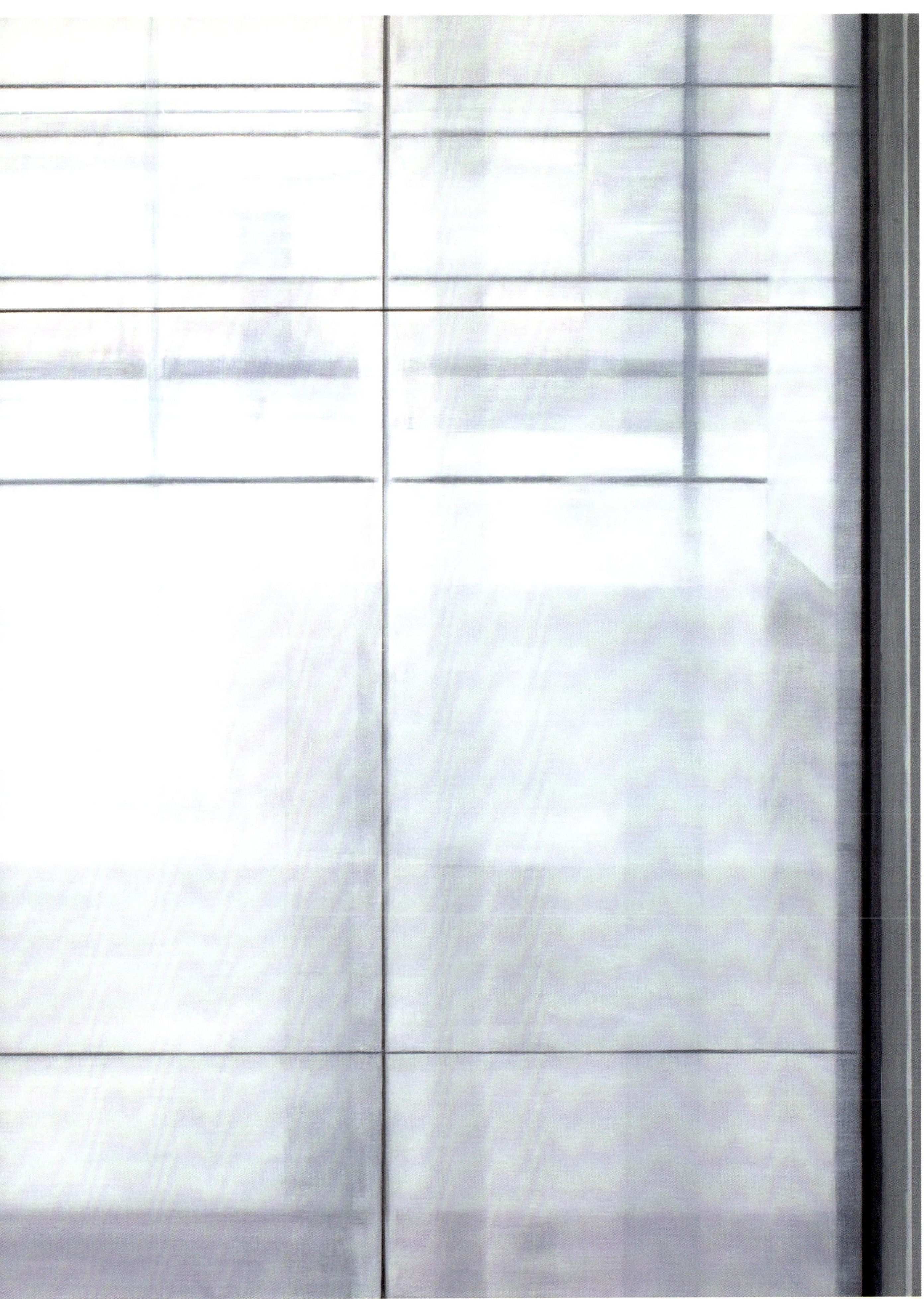

ASCERTAINING THE UNCERTAIN: BETWEEN ANYWHERE AND NOWHERE

SAYAKO MIZUTA

Is it a waving curtain that is depicted in *Kowaremono*, or is it something like the boundary between skin and clothing? The enigmatic title further adds to my confusion as to how and from what perspective to look at this painting. Am I watching the subtle movements of an organdy-like cloth from outside the building? Or am I trying to assure myself of the soft fabric's texture in a secure indoor setting? As the title suggests, the painting shows something brittle and fragile, but I realize that it displays at once also the flexibility and inner richness of weak and ephemeral things.

Miwa Ogasawara uses subdued oil colors to depict such vague and intangible subjects as light, shadow, wind, and air. Motifs that repeatedly appear in her paintings include indoor spaces, vessels, glass balls, bodies of young or adolescent boys and girls, and landscapes with trees or watersides. These things quietly dwell at places that could be anywhere and nowhere, at an indeterminate time somewhere between day and night. These illusionary sceneries beyond time and space inspire me to imagine things like a child's room full of toys; a place where one can retreat after something bad happened; secretly weeping under a blanket; the inside of the shark[1] that swallowed Pinocchio; or the basement where Nick Bowen is trapped.[2] All of these are seemingly places between here and somewhere else, like waiting rooms one enters before proceeding to the next stage. The time in these waiting rooms is a subjective one that does not flow from the past toward the future, and

VON DER ERKENNTNIS EINER UNBESTIMMTEN RAUMZEITLICHEN ILLUSION

Was ist auf dem Bild Kowaremono (Zerbrechlichkeit) *zu sehen? Ist es ein flirrender Vorhang oder das Dazwischen zwischen Haut und Kleidungsstück? Nicht nur der Titel bleibt rätselhaft, ich bin mir auch nicht sicher, von welchem Standpunkt aus ich das Bild betrachte. Stehe ich außen vor einem Gebäude, in dem ich innen die leichten Bewegungen eines Organdy-Stoffes sehe? Oder befinde ich mich an einem sicheren Ort im Raum und befühle, um Gewissheit zu erlangen, das weiche Gewebe? So wie der Titel suggeriert, ist auf dem Bild etwas Zerbrechliches und Fragiles dargestellt, aber ich sehe auch das Zarte und Flüchtige, seine Geschmeidigkeit und seinen inneren Reichtum.*

Miwa Ogasawara malt farblich dezente Ölbilder mit schwer zu fassenden Motiven wie Licht, Schatten, Wind und Luft. Es sind immer wiederkehrende Darstellungen von Innenräumen, Gefäßen, Glaskugeln und Kindern, jungen Körpern sowie Baum- und Uferlandschaften. Diese Bilder existieren still in einer unbestimmten Zeit, wo Tag und Nacht sich mischen, an irgendwelchen universellen Orten. Die Illusion dieser nicht näher bestimmbaren Zeit-Räume weckt Assoziationen und Erinnerungen an solche Räume: an das mit geliebten Dingen vollgestellte Kinderzimmer; an Orte, an die man sich allein zurückzieht, wenn etwas Unangenehmes vorgefallen ist; an das Bett, in dem wir leise vor uns hin weinen; an den Haifischbauch, in dem Pinocchio umherirrt,[1] oder an das unterirdische Zimmer, in dem Nick Bowen sich eingeschlossen hat.[2]

どこでもない時空の幻影を認識すること

水田紗弥子

Kowaremono（こわれもの）に描かれているのはカーテンのゆらめきなのか、あるいは皮膚と衣服のあわいなのだろうか。謎めいたタイトルと共に、私はどこからこの絵を見ているのだろうと不安になる。オーガンジーのような布の微かな動きを、建物の外から眺めているのだろうか。あるいは家の中の安心した場所で、柔らかい布地の手触りを確かめようとしているのかもしれない。タイトルの表す通り、こわれやすく、脆いものが描かれているこの作品には、弱く、はかないもののしなやかさ、内的な豊かさが描かれていることにも気づかされる。

小笠原美環は、光や陰、風や空気といった曖昧で捉えどころのないモチーフを、色調を抑えた油絵で描く。繰り返し描かれるイメージは建物の室内や器やガラスの玉、思春期の少年少女や子どもの身体、樹々や水辺の風景などである。そしてこれらのイメージは、昼と夜が混ざったような不確かな時間の、どこでもないような普遍的な場所に静かに存在している。どこでもない時空の幻影は、私にこんな空間を思い起こさせる。お気に入りのもので満たされた子ども部屋、嫌なことがあったときにひとりになれる場所、静かに泣いたふとんのなか、あるいはピノキオがさまよったサメの腹のなか（註1）、ニック·ボウエンが閉じ込められた地下室（註2）。これらは、ここどこかを繋ぐ、次に向かうための待合室のような場だ。待合室には過去から未来に流れる時間ではない、主観的な時間が漂い、普段は気にも留めないような場が丁寧に描かれ、私たちはその重要さにやっと気づく。ピノキオは勇気を出してサメの腹からおじいさんを救出し、ニック·ボウエンは、窓も内側から開ける手立てもない地下室からの脱出方法を想像する。でも私たちはそこを思い切って飛び出たあと、なかなか振り返り思い出すことはない。小笠原の絵画を通じて、忘れていたその秘密基地をふいに開けてしまう。絵画に描かれたカーテンのゆらめき、窓にうつる影や、廊下や通路で感じた

the minute depictions of these kinds of places that we normally don't even take notice of finally make us realize just how important they are. Pinocchio musters up his courage to rescue the old man from the shark's belly, and Nick Bowen tries to think up ways to escape from a basement with no means of opening doors or windows from the inside. But we, once we have broken free and jumped out from such places, tend to not look back. It is through Ogasawara's paintings that the entranceways to those forgotten secret bases are suddenly opened. When we stand in front of the paintings and relive the experience of waving curtains, the silhouettes in the windows, the lights in the aisles and corridors, we feel how emotions that have been untouched for a long time are gradually unlocked.

Once again, I fix my eyes on the clear glass balls that are the subjects of the *Glaskugel* series. Each painting captures a moment in which the respective spherical object looks as if it were about to start rolling, while the light and the environment it is placed in are vaguely reflected in its surface. The presence of a transparent glass ball is highlighted the moment someone touches and moves it, or when the light is switched on and illuminates it. It's an object that is free to go anywhere and to reflect any scenery on its surface, but the fact that its surroundings define its presence also hints at the hardships of not being able to exist independently. It can be understood as a symbol of fragility and unstableness, as it may accidentally roll away and break at any time.

The air particles depicted in *Inbetween* appear to be lost somewhere between the starting and ending points of a journey from a station toward an unknown destination. Maybe they are free to go where they like, but maybe they are at once so weak that they are easily swept away. *Zwischenraum 8* depicts a window with masking tape on it. The interval between the completion of a building's construction and the time someone moves in is like an idle, temporary void in space and time that is quietly marked by this *X*.

Es sind Orte, die eine Verbindung von hier nach irgendwo schlagen, einem Wartezimmer ähnlich, von dem aus es zur nächsten Station geht. In Wartezimmern fließt die Zeit nicht von der Vergangenheit zur Zukunft hin, in ihnen herrscht eine subjektive Zeit. Es sind sorgfältig gemalte Orte, denen wir für gewöhnlich keine Beachtung schenken, deren Bedeutung wir uns aber endlich bewusst werden. Mutig rettet Pinocchio sich und den alten Geppetto aus dem Haifischbauch, und Nick Bowen ersinnt eine Methode, um dem unterirdischen Zimmer, dessen Fenster sich von innen nicht öffnen lassen, zu entfliehen. Doch kaum sind wir mit einem Satz herausgesprungen, erinnern wir uns nicht mehr, wir drehen uns nicht einmal mehr um. Dank der Bilder von Ogasawara aber öffnen sich unerwartet die in Vergessenheit geratenen, geheimen Basislager. Wir stehen vor den Bildern und erleben noch einmal das Flirren der Vorhänge, die im Fenster reflektierenden Schatten, das Licht, das wir im Korridor oder im Durchgang spürten. Gefühlswelten tun sich auf, an die wir schon lange nicht mehr gerührt haben.

Ich wende mich der Serie Glaskugel *zu, Bildern, auf denen durchsichtige Glaskugeln gemalt sind, in denen sich verschwommen die Landschaften und Lichtverhältnisse spiegeln, in denen sie eingebettet liegen, eingefroren in dem Moment, da sie wegrollen oder sich bewegen könnten. Die durchsichtige Glaskugel existiert dann, wenn jemand sie berührt und bewegt oder das Licht einschaltet und sie so beleuchtet. Sie kann alles spiegeln und überallhin rollen, doch da die Umgebung ihre Existenz bestimmt, symbolisiert sie zugleich ein Leben, das niemals frei ist. Sie steht für die Flüchtigkeit, das Wissen, dass jederzeit etwas ins Rollen geraten und zerbrechen kann. Auf dem Bild* Inbetween *erinnern die sphärischen Lichtblasen an Personen, die verloren im Bahnhof stehen, sie haben weder ein Ziel, noch wissen sie, wann sie abfahren oder ankommen werden. Sie können kommen und gehen, wie sie wollen, aber vielleicht werden sie auch fortgetrieben, so labil ist ihre Existenz.*

光を絵画の前で追体験するとき、長い時間触れていなかった感情が開いていくのを感じる。

改めて、透明なガラスの球体が描かれる*Glaskugel*（ガラス玉）シリーズに目を留めてみる。球体が置かれた場の風景や光が、ガラス玉にぼんやりと写り、転がり動きだしそうな一瞬が閉じ込められている。透明なガラスの球は、誰かが触って動かしたとき、電気をつけて光をうけたときに、その存在が浮かび上がってくる。なんでも写すことができ、どこにでも行ける存在でもあるが、周囲の環境が存在を規定していくということは、自由ではいられない生きづらさの表象でもある。そして、思いがけず転がり、あっけなく壊れてしまう儚い表象にも受け取れる。*Inbetween*（あいま）に描かれる大気の粒は、駅舎にいながら目的地がなく、出発と到着の間のどちらでもない迷子のようだ。自由に往来できるようで、流されていってしまう弱い存在でもあるかもしれない。*Zwischenraum 8*（間の空間 8）に描かれるのは、建物の窓に貼られたマスキングテープ。工事が終わり、誰かが建物を使い始めるまでの隙間は、宙に浮いて刻まれない時空間のようだ。ばつ印が私たちにその存在を静かに知らせてくれる。

ところが複雑な感情や不確かな時空にまるで覚えがなく、自由さと生きにくさを兼ねた存在である自分にも心当たりがない人が多くいる。人間は、科学技術の発達により、自然科学の事象の外側に立って、それをコントロールできる立場になったと思い込んでいる節がある。そして科学を唯一の真理と勘違いをすることで、説明しきれない曖昧な感覚、偶然に起こった出来事や、不条理などに向き合えずにいる。近年、人工知能やバーチャルリアリティなどの発達、オルタナティブファクトやディープフェイクなど、私たちの想像していた近未来図を超えた超現実が立ち上がってきた。そして不寛容や想像力の欠如が原因と形容されるさまざまな事案が私たちを日々、落ち込ませる。

一見するとシンプルだが、内面のささやかな変化や存在の曖昧さが表れる小笠原の絵を観ることは、新たな関係を見つけ自分なりの解を得るための鍛錬となる。鑑賞と経験を重ねると、自然科学では導き出せない解に向き合うこととなるからだ。例えば、静かなイメージだが内面の葛藤やゆらぎを絵画に見つけ対峙していると、主流な考えに抗い、異なる道筋にジャンプする力が蓄えられていく。また、通路のような器のような絵画を繰り返し見ていると、私たちの身体や感覚のしなやかさと強さに気づかされる。小笠原の作品に描かれている空間は、自分の存在や感情に深く結びついているが、描かれる空間を規定しているのは

A lot of people, however, have no recollection whatsoever of complicated feelings or uncertain times and spaces, and no understanding of their lives as involving both liberties and hardships. We humans tend to believe that technical developments have put us in a position where we look at natural scientific phenomena from the outside and even control them. The misunderstanding of science as the one and only truth makes us unable to deal with vague and not entirely explicable sensations, accidental occurrences, and things that defy logic. With the advance of artificial intelligence, virtual reality, alternative facts and deep fakes, a hyper-reality has emerged in recent years that exceeds the picture that we used to have of the near future. Day by day, there is an array of cases in which we are dragged into depression as a result of intolerance and lacking imagination.

Ogasawara's paintings may look simple at a glance, but the observation of the subtle inner transformations and the vagueness of existence that they express is a training in discovering new relationships for the viewer in the search of his or her own personal solutions. That is because the repeated appreciation and experience of these works present us with clues that natural sciences cannot provide. Finding and confronting the inner conflicts and fluctuations that are there, even in the quiet images, charges us with the power to resist established ideas and to jump onto different trains. When repeatedly looking at the paintings that seem to show things like corridors, or maybe vessels, one is reminded of the flexibility and strength of the human body and senses. While the spaces depicted in Ogasawara's works are closely linked to aspects of existence and emotion, what specifies the painted spaces are the surrounding social, political, historical, and cultural circumstances of our time. We can also read in them matters that have been arising as results of various forms of division, such as refugees, immigration, and racial and sexual discrimination, as well as the collision with

Auf dem Bild Zwischenraum 8 *sehen wir ein Fenster, dessen Ränder mit Kreppband abgeklebt sind. Die Bauarbeiten sind beendet, aber noch ist niemand eingezogen, es ist ein Zwischenraum, ein Zeitraum, in dem die Zeit stillsteht, wie in der Luft hängt. Das große »X« auf der Glasscheibe bringt uns dessen Existenz sanft zu Bewusstsein.*

Doch viele Menschen haben weder eine Erinnerung an komplizierte Gefühlslagen oder ungewisse Zeiträume noch eine Vorstellung von ihrer von der Freiheit und den damit einhergehenden Mühen geprägten Existenz. Sie glauben, der Mensch stehe aufgrund des technologischen Fortschritts außerhalb der naturwissenschaftlichen Erscheinungen und habe alles unter Kontrolle. Sie halten die Wissenschaft fälschlicherweise für die einzige Wahrheit und sind unfähig, sich mit nicht erklärbaren und vagen Sinneswahrnehmungen, Zufallsereignissen oder widersinnigen Vorkommnissen auseinanderzusetzen. Andererseits ist durch die Entwicklung von künstlicher Intelligenz und virtueller Realität, von alternative facts und deep fake eine Superrealität entstanden, die unsere Vorstellung übersteigt. Wenn dann noch fehlende Toleranz und Vorstellungskraft unser tägliches Miteinander bestimmen, schlägt das unweigerlich aufs Gemüt.

Auf den ersten Blick wirken Ogasawaras Bilder schlicht, doch wenn wir die darin zum Ausdruck gebrachten subtilen Gefühlsmodulationen und Ambivalenzen des Seins erkennen, können sie uns als Übung dienen, um neue Zusammenhänge zu entdecken und zu eigenen Lösungen zu finden. Durch wiederholtes Betrachten und Wahrnehmen gelangen wir zu einer Lösung, welche die Naturwissenschaft nicht gewährleisten kann. Entdecken wir beispielsweise auf einem dieser stillen Bilder die darin dargestellten inneren Konflikte und Schwankungen, werden wir, dem allgemeinen Eindruck zum Trotz, alles daran setzen, um gedanklich auf einen neuen Weg zu gelangen. Betrachten wir wiederholt ein Bild, auf dem ein Durchgang oder ein Gefäß dargestellt ist, kann das dazu führen, dass wir uns

現在の社会情勢、政治や歴史、文化など私たちを取り巻く環境や背景である。さまざまな分断から生じる難民や移民、人種差別や性差の問題と、それへの抵抗と衝突を私たちは読み解くこともできる。しかしそれらをそのまま描くことが絵画の役割ではないことを小笠原は知っている。画家は、小説家ではないし、建築家でもない。設計をすることも、物語の筋道をつくることもしないが、鑑賞者は作品から設計図を描けるし、物語を紡ぐことができるのではないだろうか。絵画、いや美術における言葉を超えた物語が、知覚そのものや異なる時空系列を同時に表出できることに小笠原の作品を通じて出会い、私たちは感覚を修練し新たな現実に接続していく。

この論考は*RealTokyo*の掲載記事（2018年10月18日公開）をもとに加筆修正いたしました。

註1　カルロ·コッローディ『ピノッキオの冒険』大岡玲訳、2016、光文社文庫

註2　ポール·オースターの小説『オラクル·ナイト』に登場する人物で、地下室に閉じ込められてしまい脱出できないまま現在に至る。

and resistance against them. But Ogasawara is well aware that it is not the role of painting to merely reflect these things as they are. A painter is neither a novelist nor an architect. A painter does not construct buildings or storylines, but viewers can draw their own plans or compose narratives based on paintings. Ogasawara's works introduce us to the potential of narratives beyond the language of painting—or rather, of art in general—to express human perception itself and different space-time systems at the same time, to train our senses in order to connect to new realities.

This essay was written and edited based on an article that originally appeared in October 2018 on *RealTokyo*.

1 The author refers to a Japanese edition of Carlo Collodi's *The Adventures of Pinocchio*, for which Akira Ooka translated the original Italian word *monstro* into the Japanese *same* (shark).

2 Nick Bowen, a character in Paul Auster's novel *Oracle Night*, gets trapped in a basement from which he remains unable to escape.

unserer körperlichen und emotionalen Flexibilität und Stärke bewusst werden. Der Raum in Ogasawaras Bildern ist eng mit unserer Existenz und unseren Gefühlen verbunden, doch dieser gemalte Raum ist bestimmt von unserer Umwelt: der aktuellen gesellschaftlichen Lage, von Politik, Geschichte und Kultur. Wir können aus den Bildern sogar diverse soziale Konflikte herauslesen: Probleme wie die der Flüchtlings- und Einwanderungspolitik, der Rassen- und Geschlechterdiskriminierung, aber wir sehen auch den Widerstand und das Aufbegehren dagegen. Doch Ogasawara weiß, dass es nicht die Aufgabe der Künstler ist, solche Problematiken eins zu eins ins Bild zu setzen. Maler sind nicht Schriftsteller oder Architekten. Sie zeichnen keine Pläne und denken sich keine Geschichten aus, aber vielleicht können die Betrachter vom Bild ausgehend einen Entwurf oder eine Geschichte entwickeln. In der Begegnung mit Ogasawaras Werk erfahren wir, wie Geschichten, welche die Sprache der Malerei und sogar der Kunst übersteigen, die Wahrnehmung als solche sowie eine anders geartete raumzeitliche Ordnung auszudrücken vermögen, und so treten wir, vermittels dieser Schulung unserer Sinneswahrnehmung, mit einer neuen Wirklichkeit in Kontakt.

1 *Carlo Collodi,* Le avventure di Pinocchio, *1881–83.*

2 *Nick Bowen ist eine Figur aus Paul Austers Roman* Nacht des Orakels, *die in einem unterirdischen Zimmer lebt, dem sie nicht zu entkommen vermag.*

p. 66 *19.06 / 2019*
37 × 27 cm / Gouache on paper

p. 68 *19.05 / 2019*
38.5 × 27.5 cm / Gouache on paper

p. 71 *19.07 / 2019*
37 × 26 cm / Gouache on paper

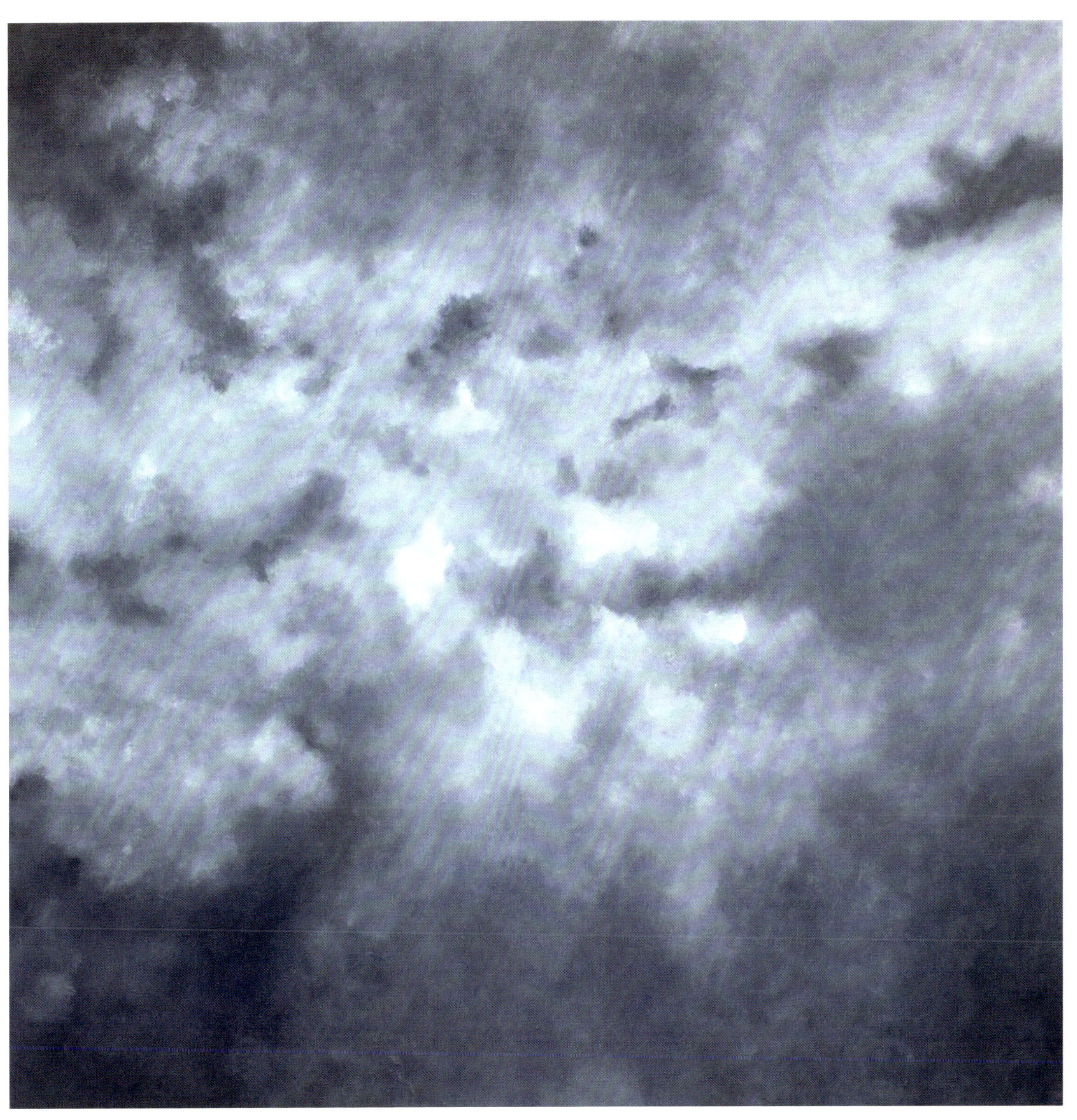

NATUR 2019 / 120 × 120 cm

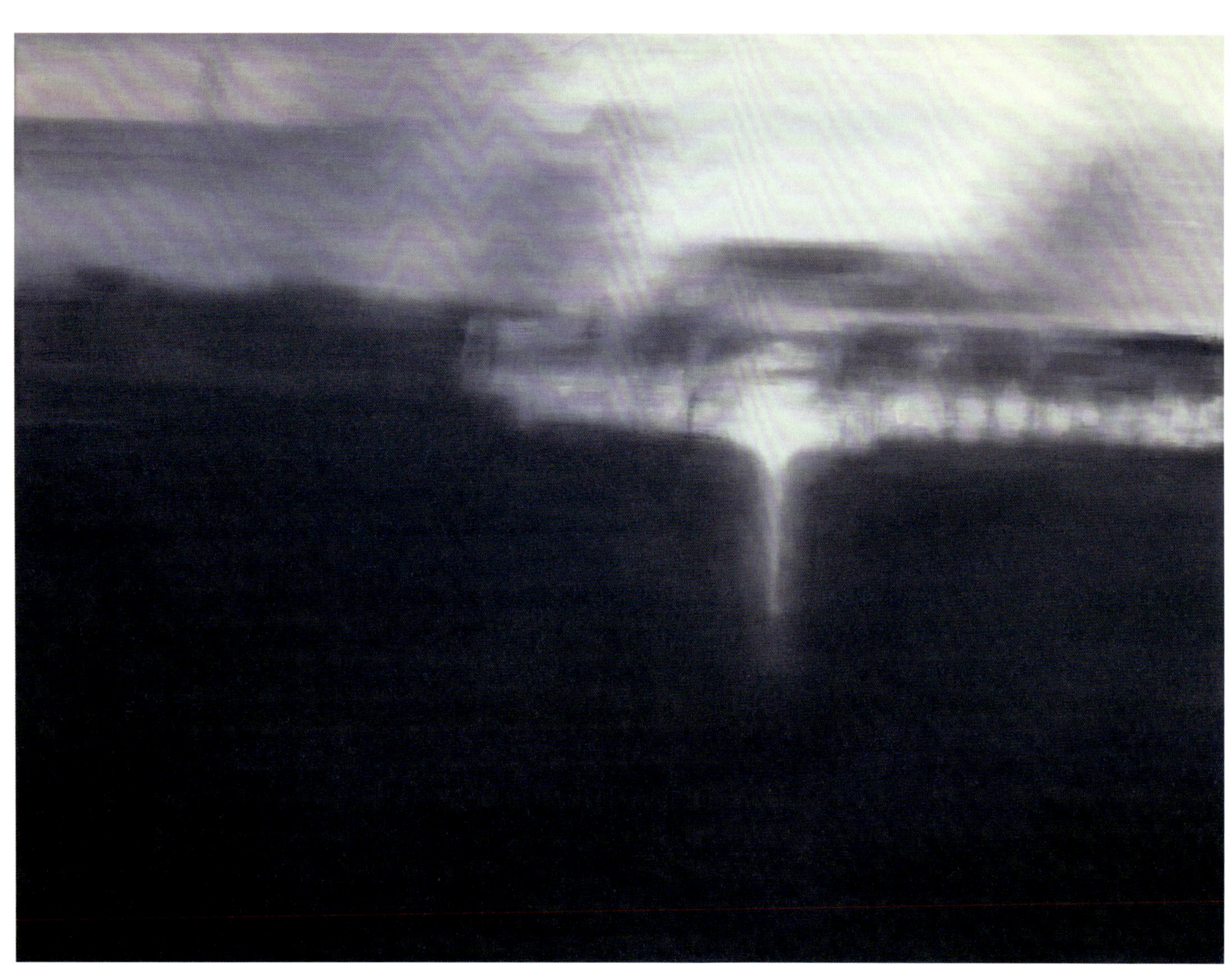

 LAND 2 2018 / 120 × 160 cm

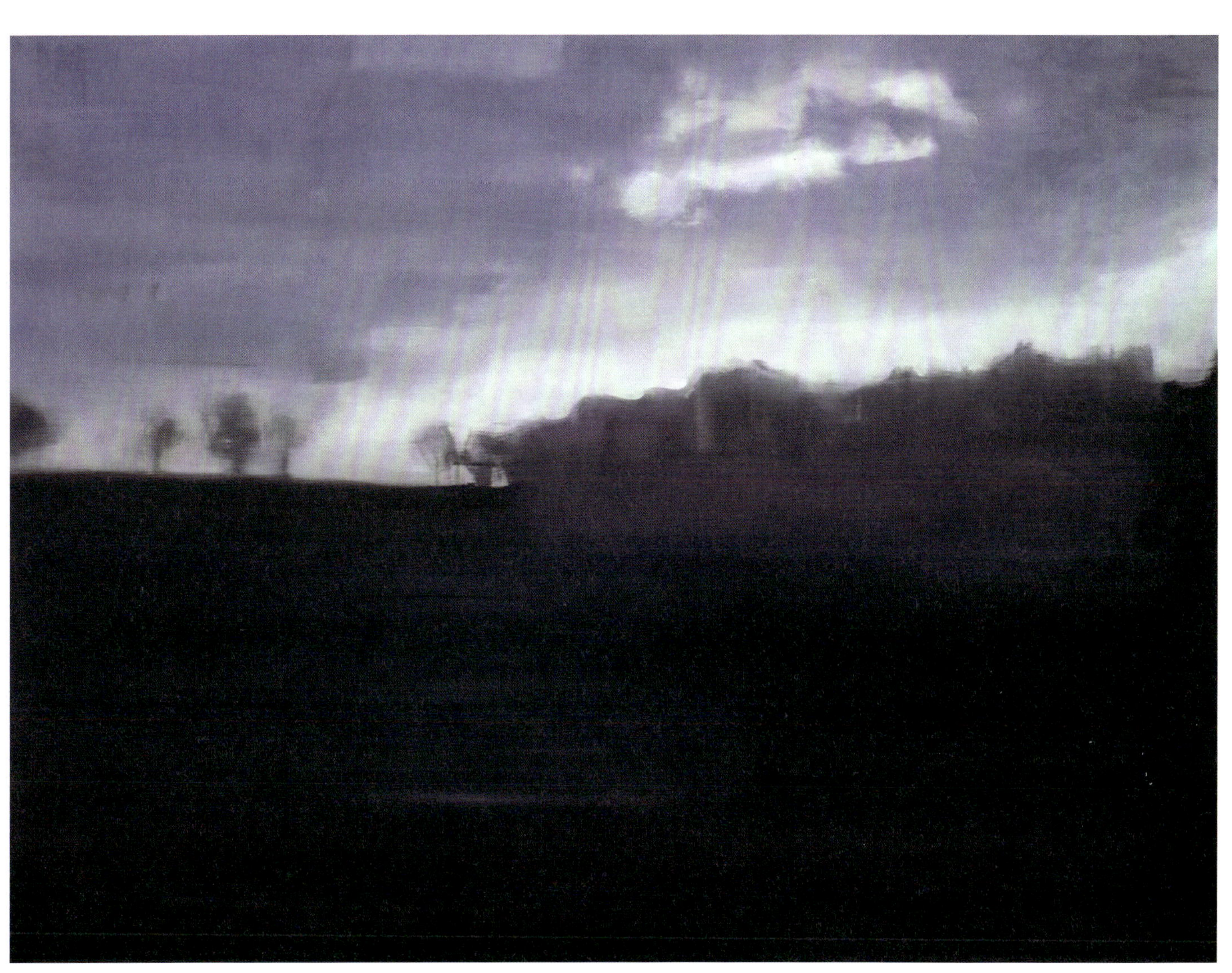

LAND 3 2018 / 120 × 160 cm LAND 1 > 2018 / 120 × 160 cm

LICHTERMEER 2019 / 130 × 110 cm

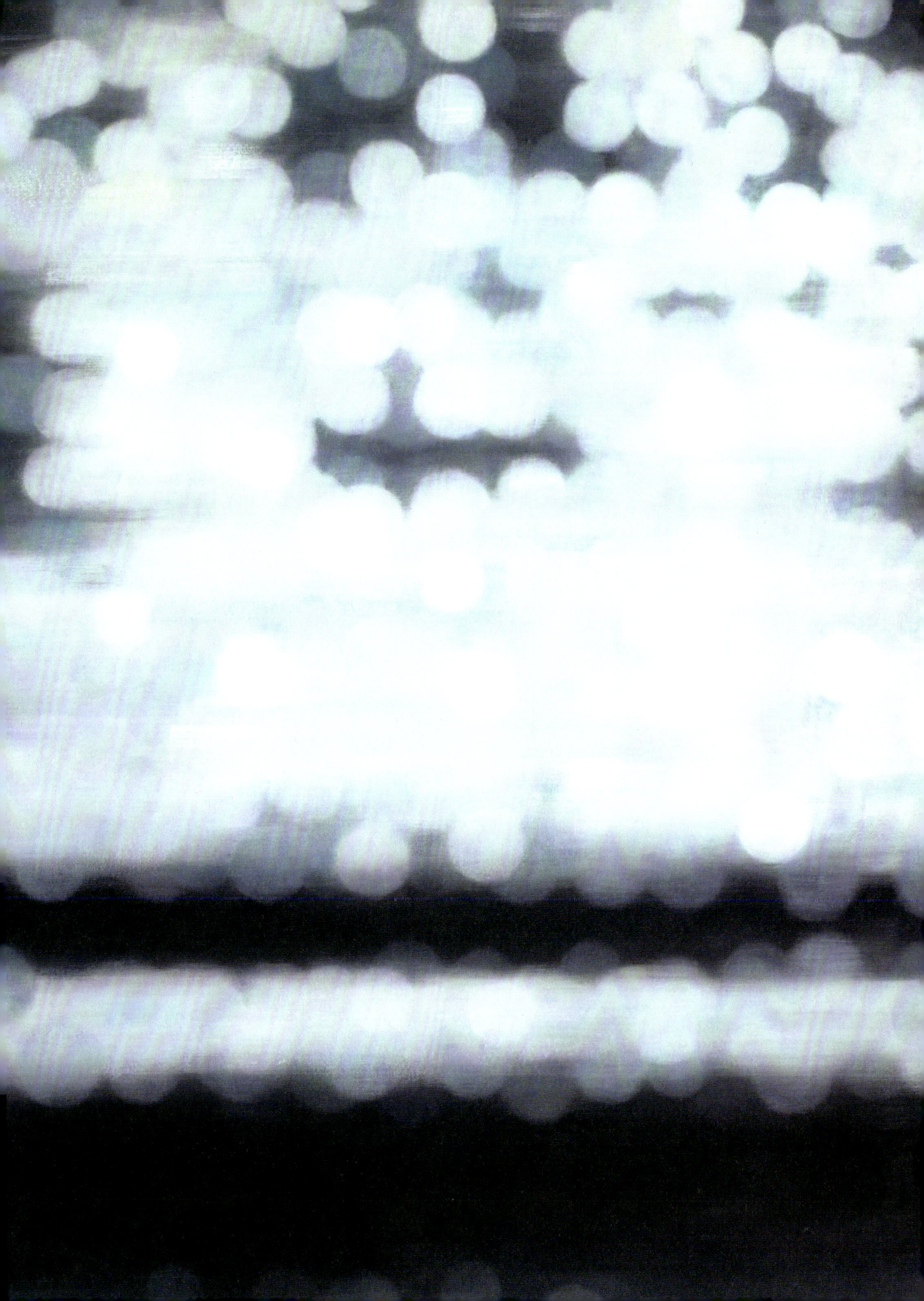

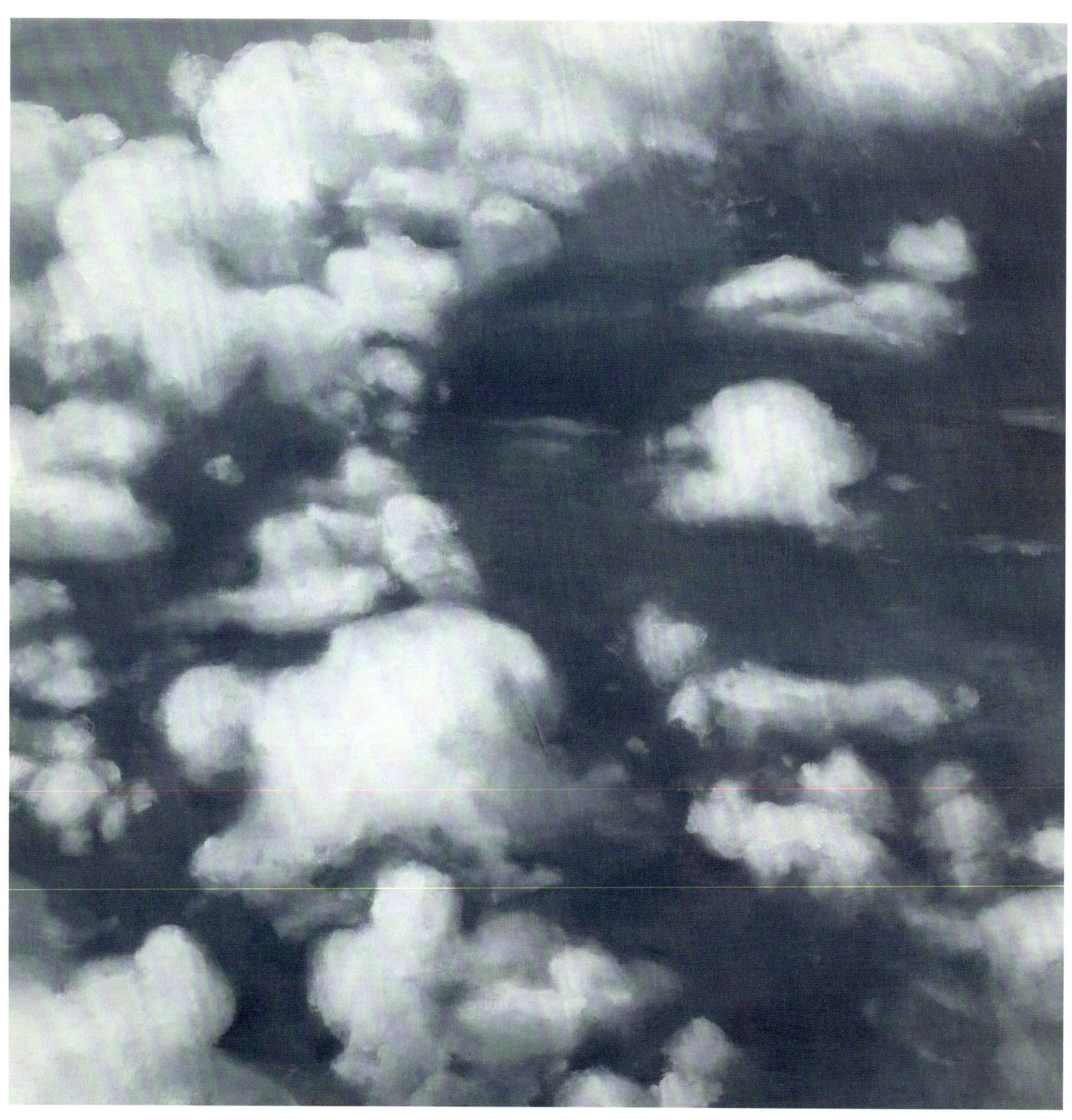

 ABOVE 1 2016 / 70 × 70 cm

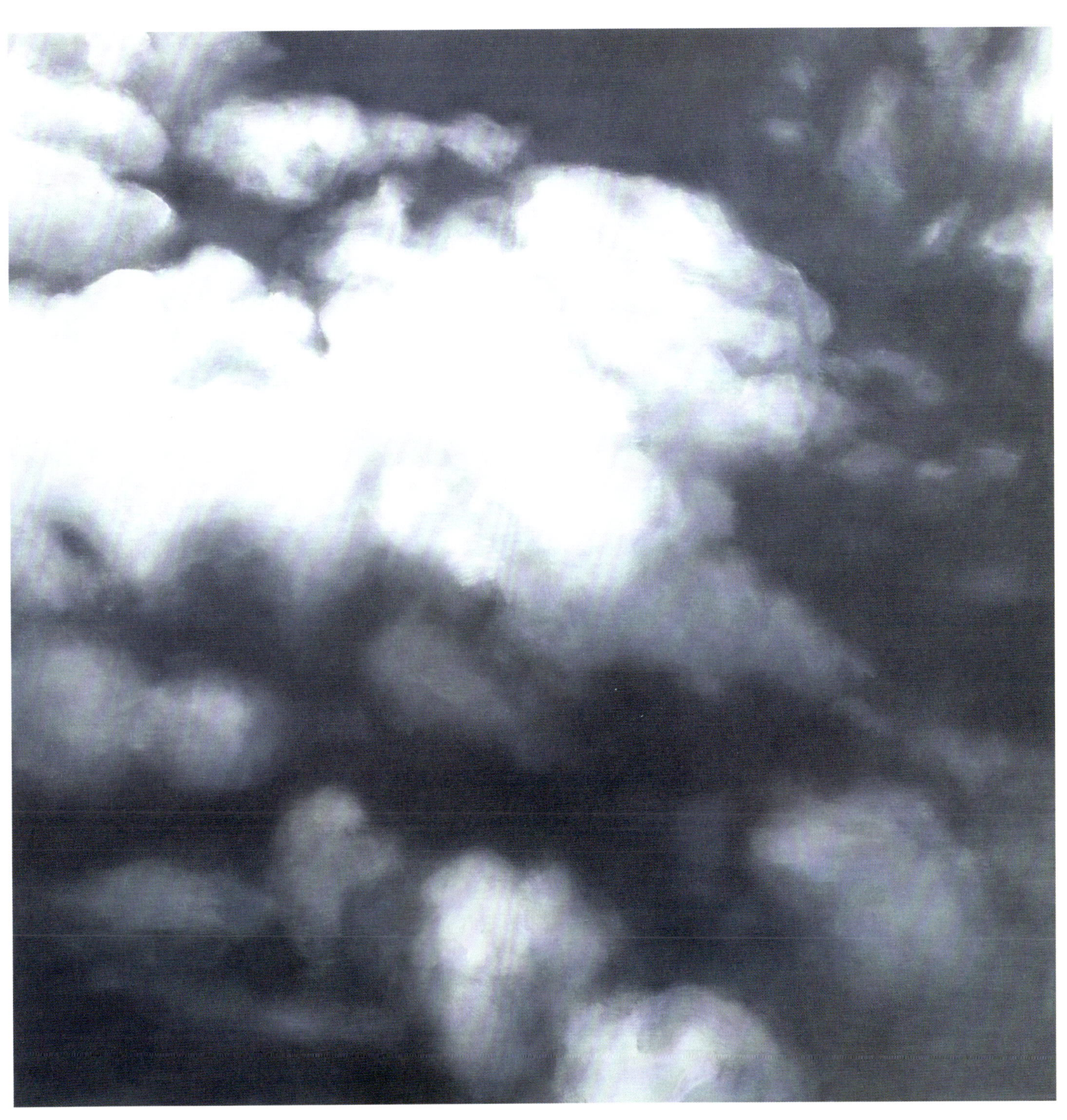

ABOVE 2 2016 / 70 × 70 cm

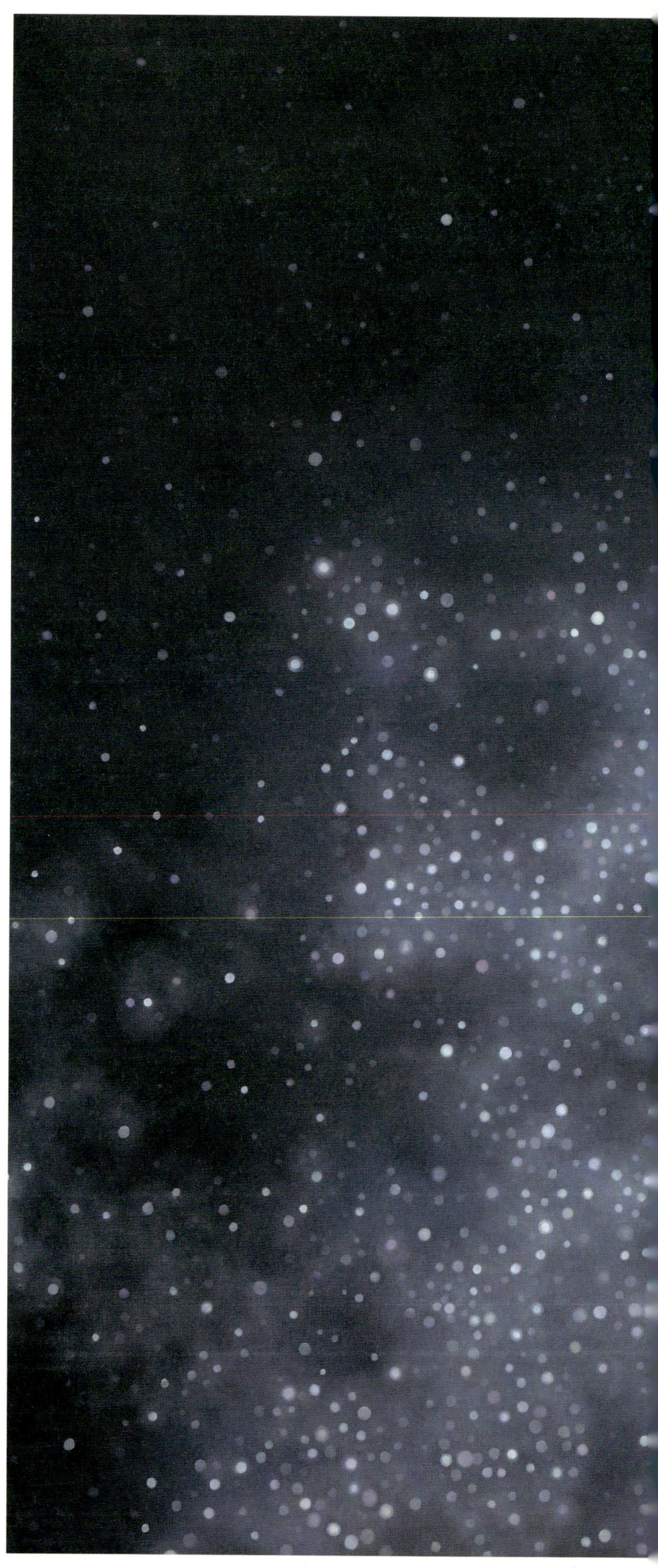

 WELTBILD 2 2019 / 150 × 190 cm

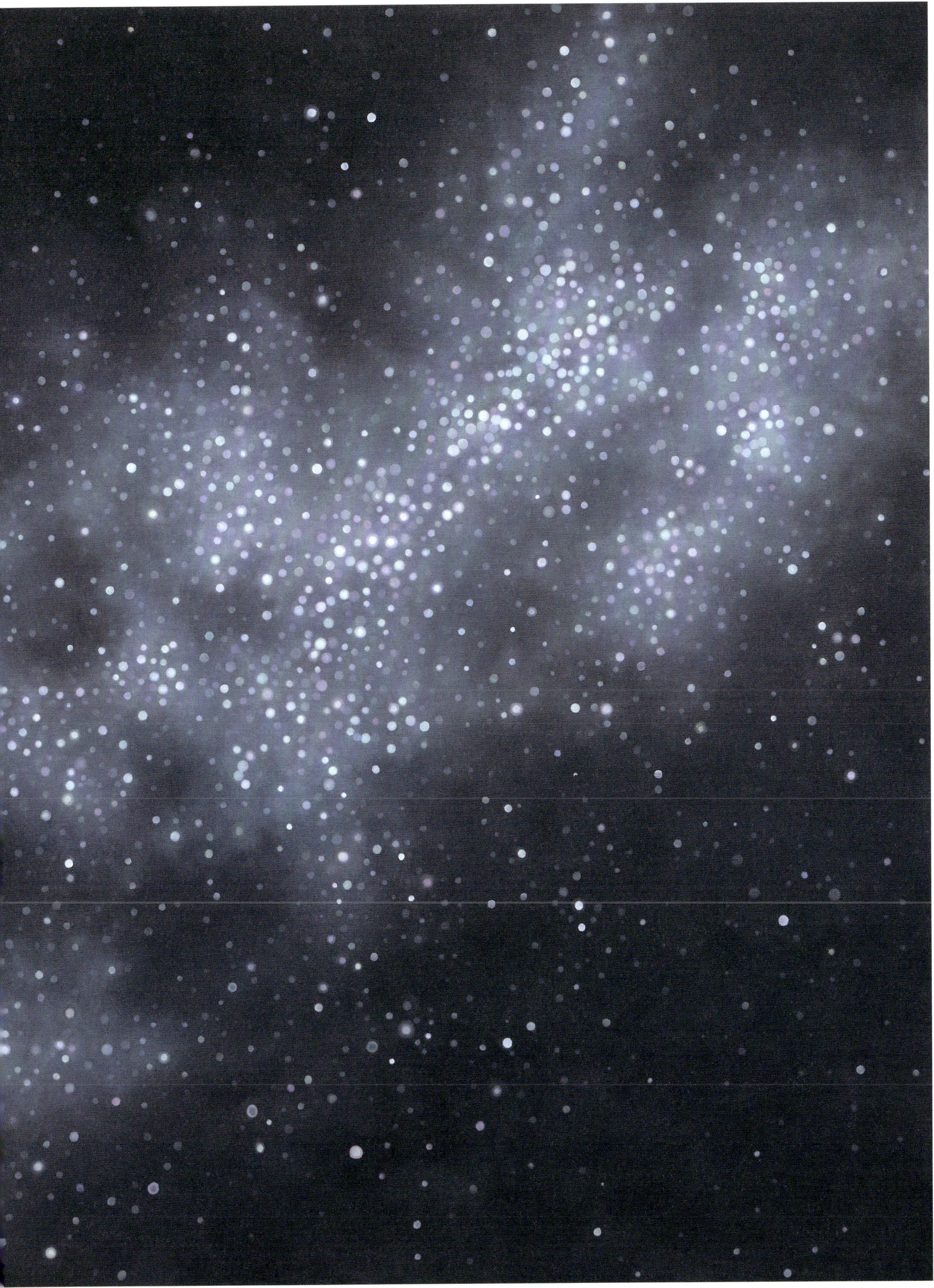

HARU 2017 / 100 × 70 cm

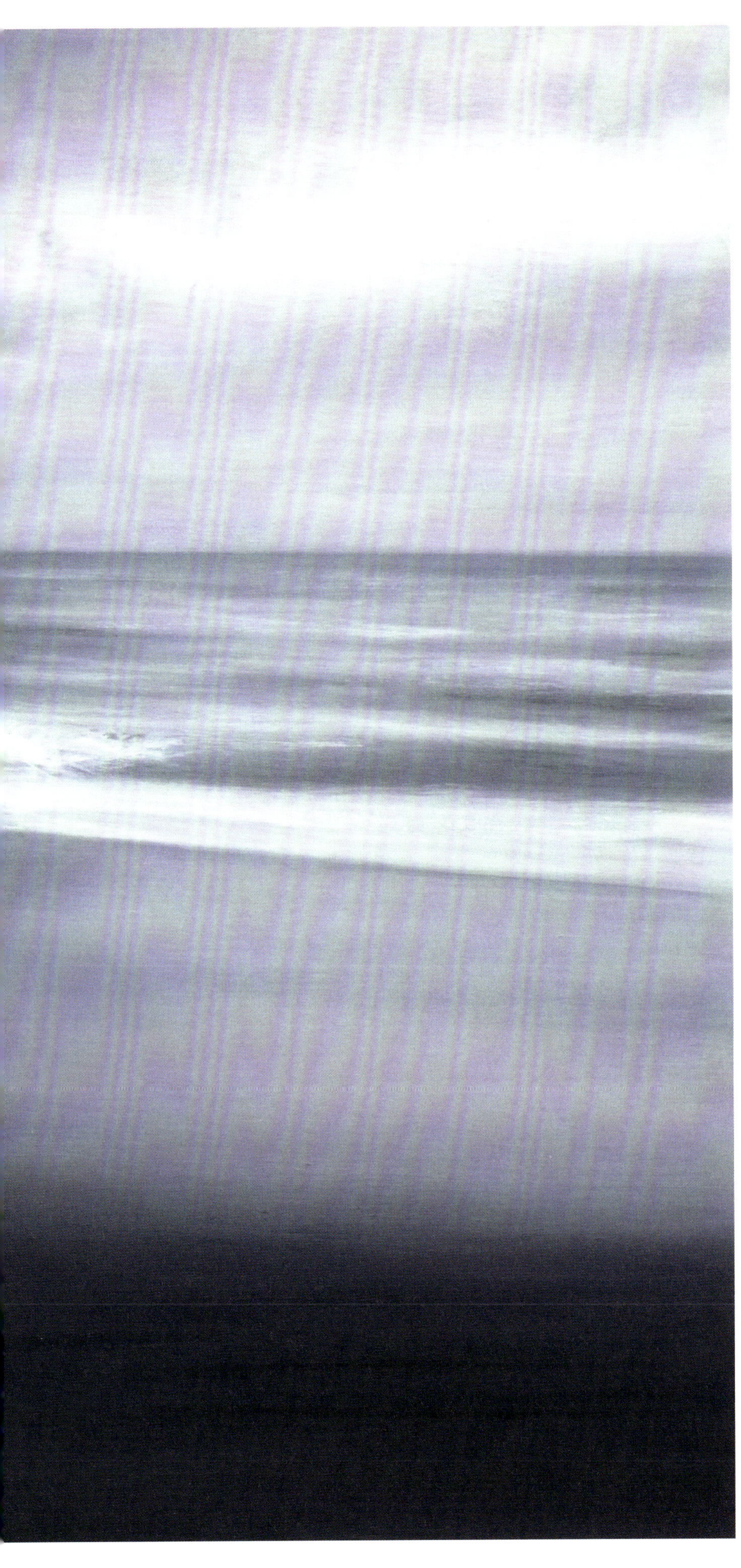

HORIZON 2018 / 120 × 160 cm

 HORIZON 1 2019 / 80 × 100 cm

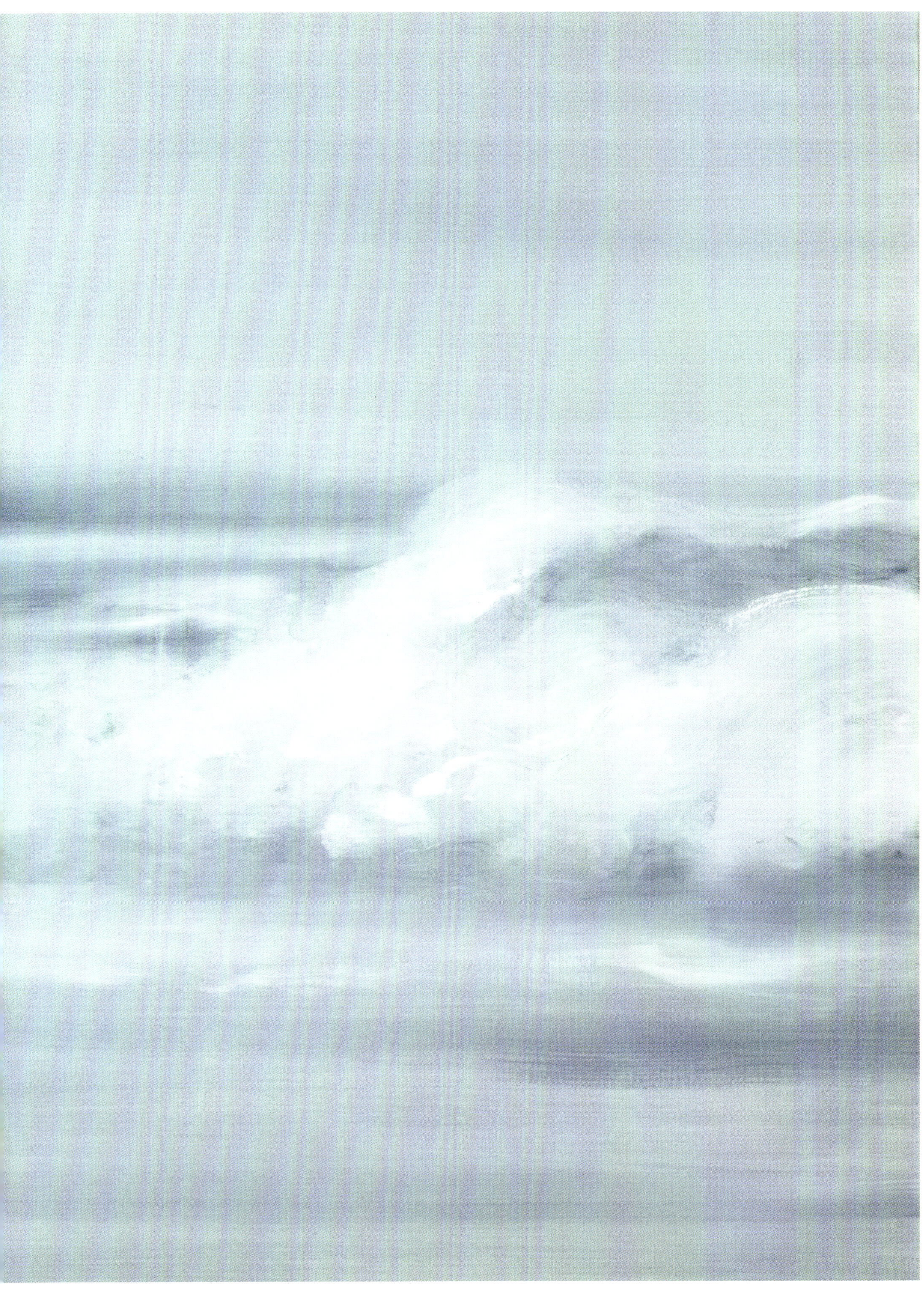

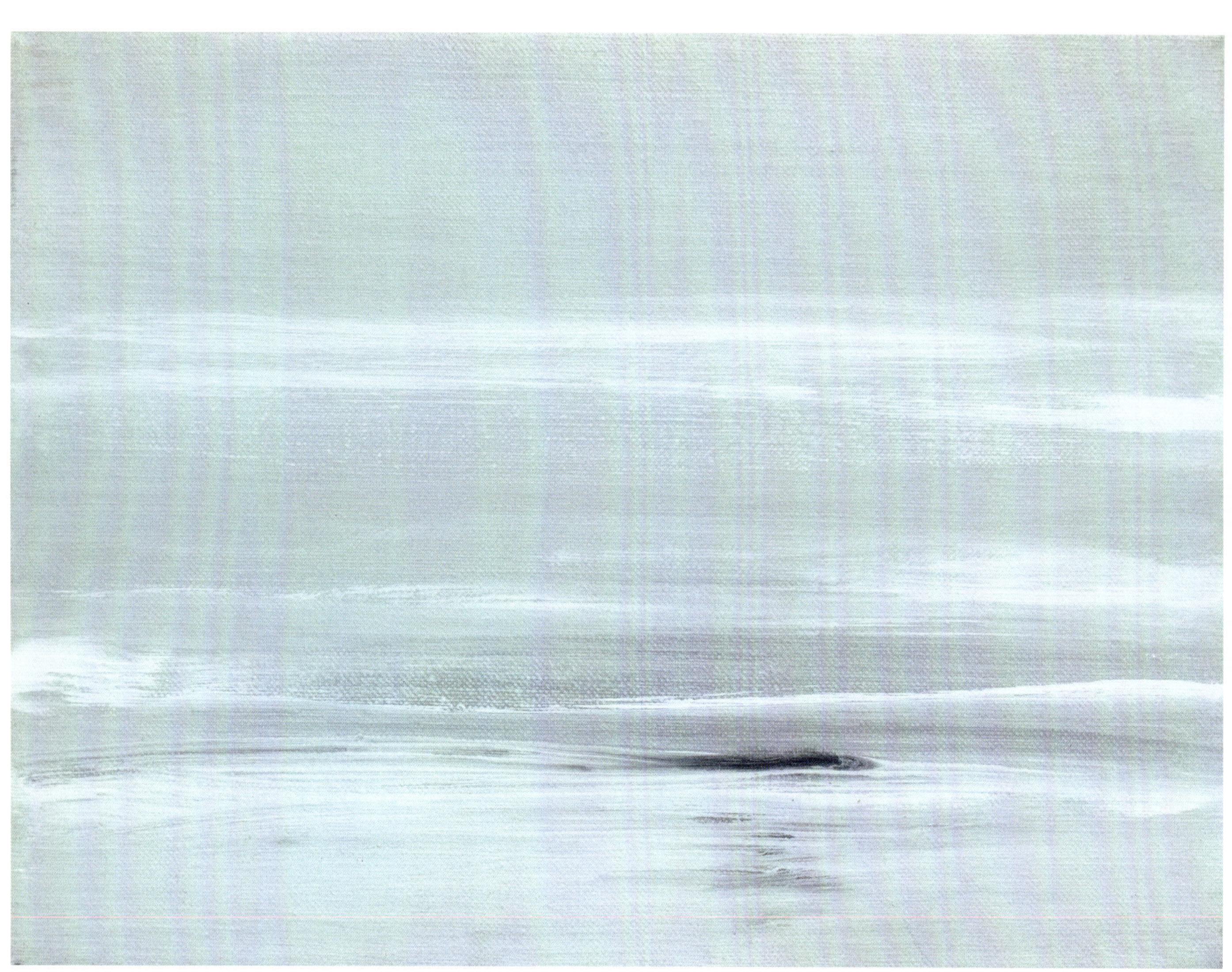

 OCEAN 3 2015 / 30 × 40 cm

OCEAN 4 2015 / 30 × 40 cm BIRDS > 2017 / 180 × 140 cm + 180 × 150 cm

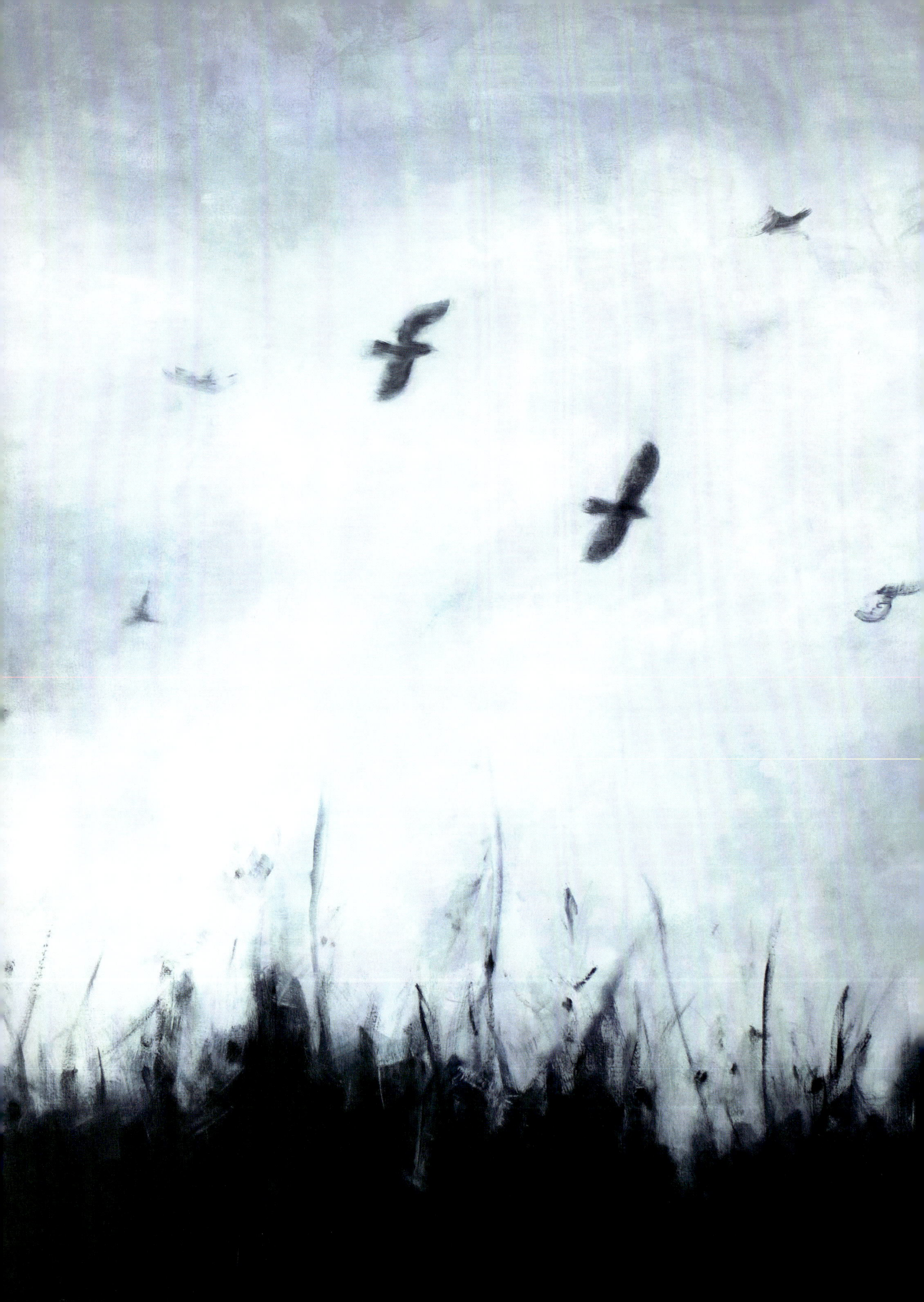

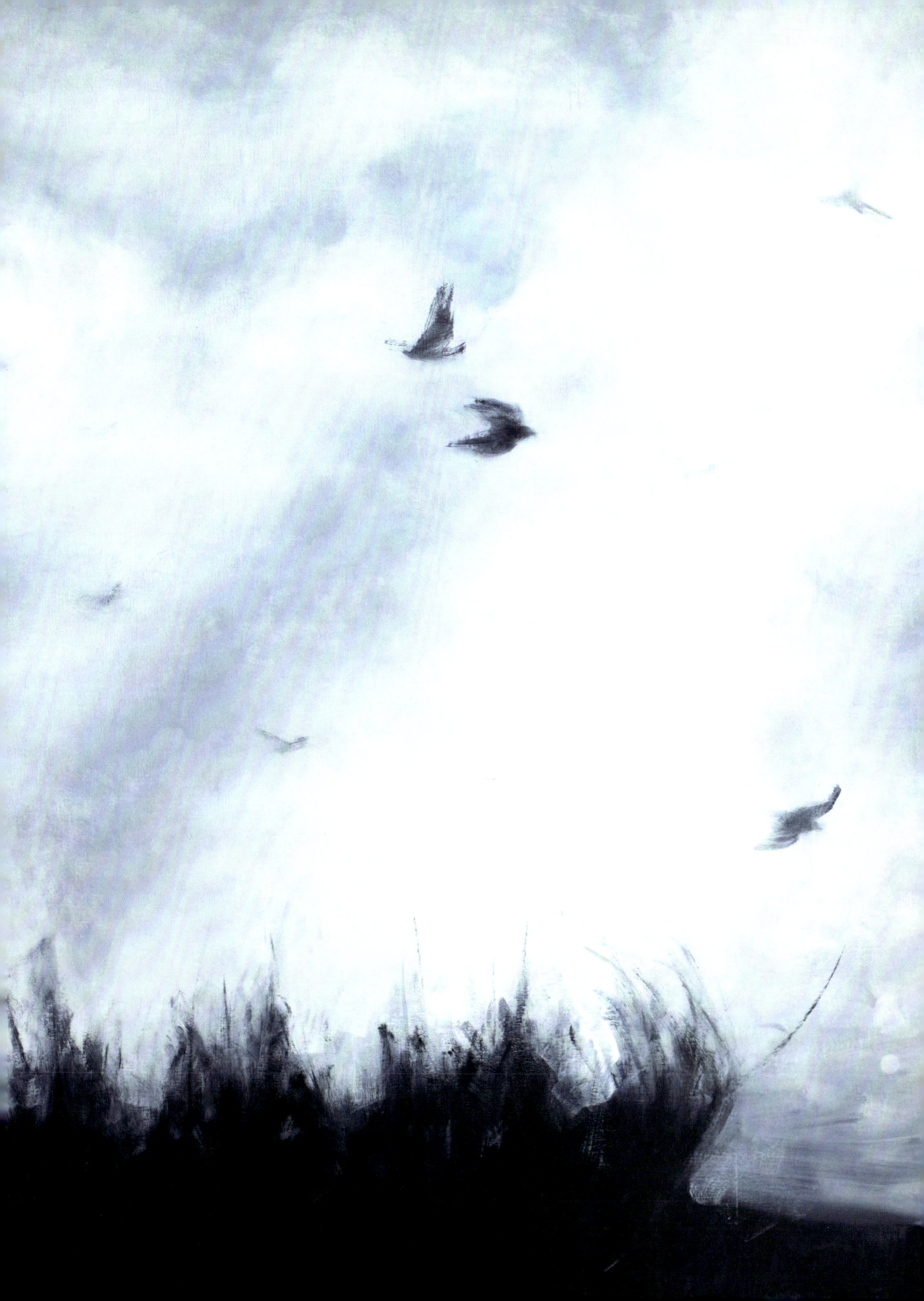

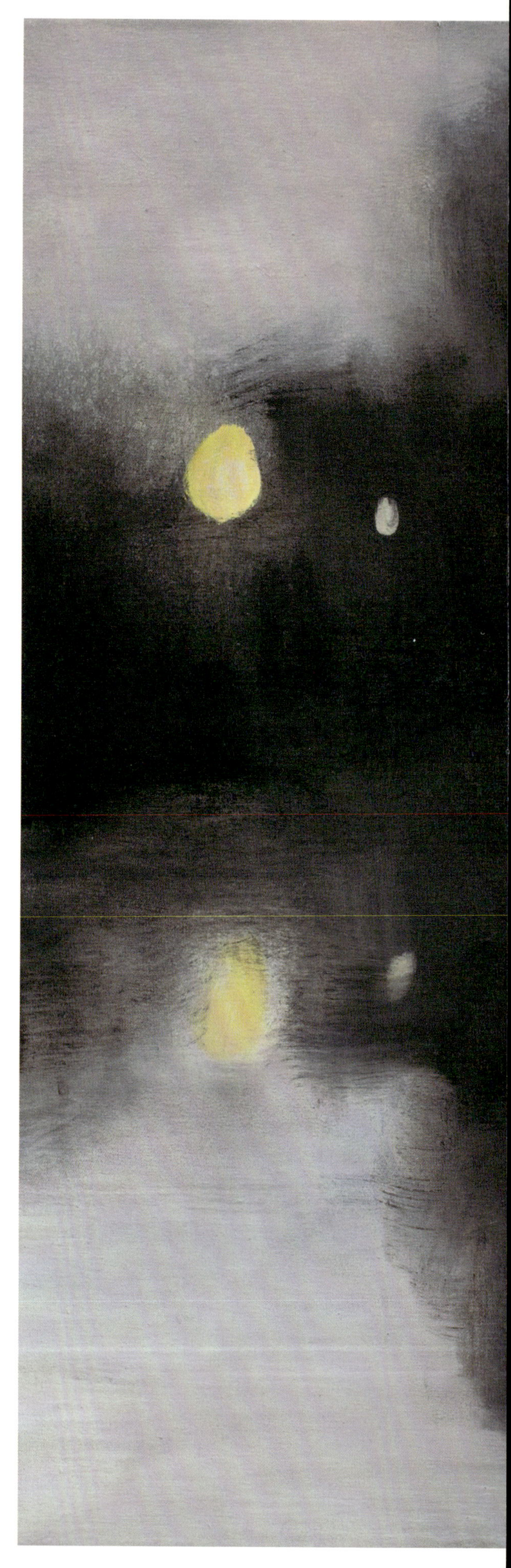

 HEIMWEG 2006 / 60 × 70 cm

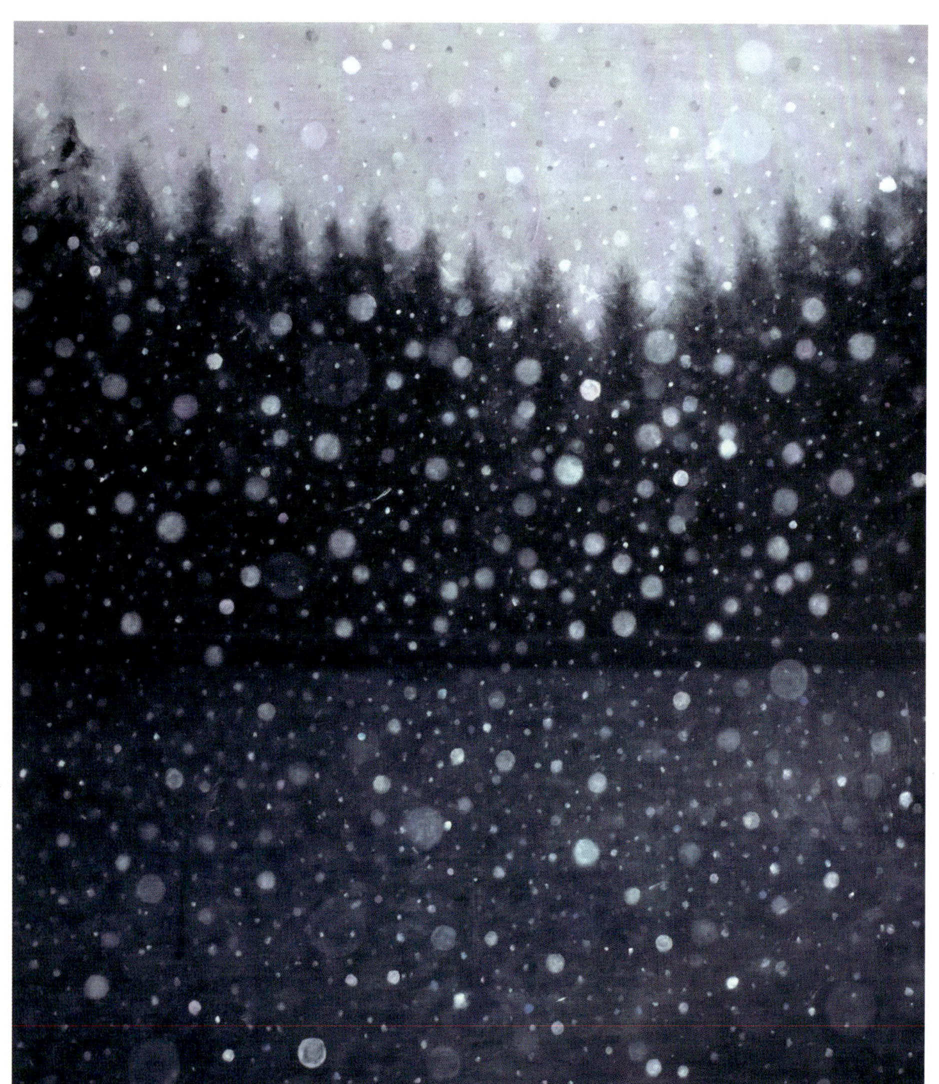

 BORDER 2017 / triptych / 160 × 140 cm, 160 × 160 cm, 160 × 140 cm

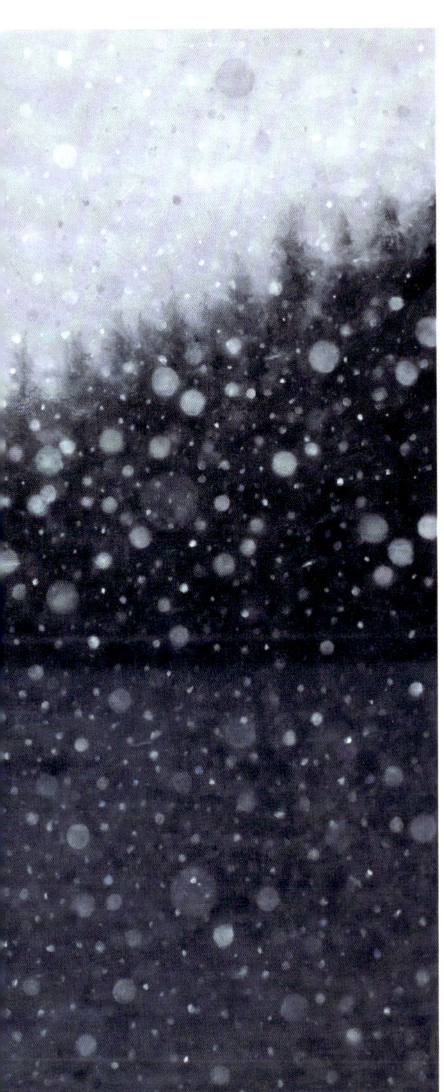
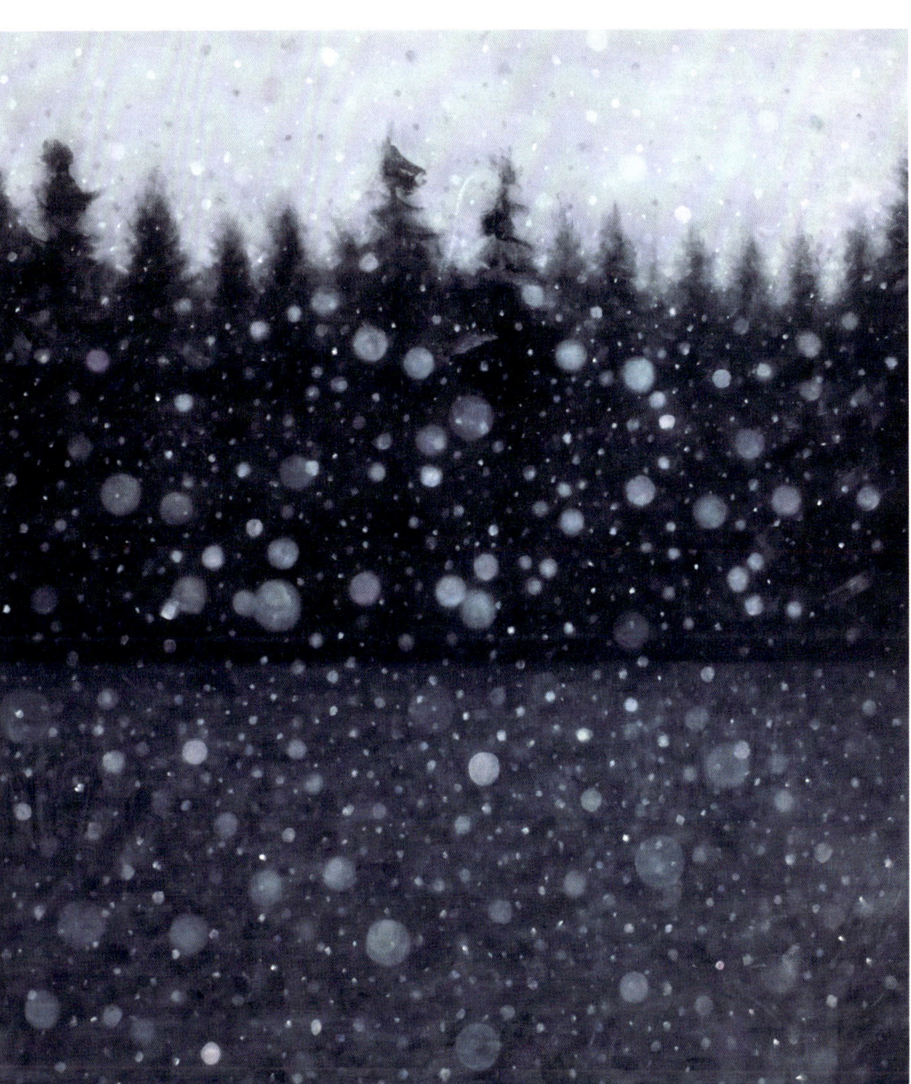

WELTBILD 4 > 2019 / 170 × 240 cm

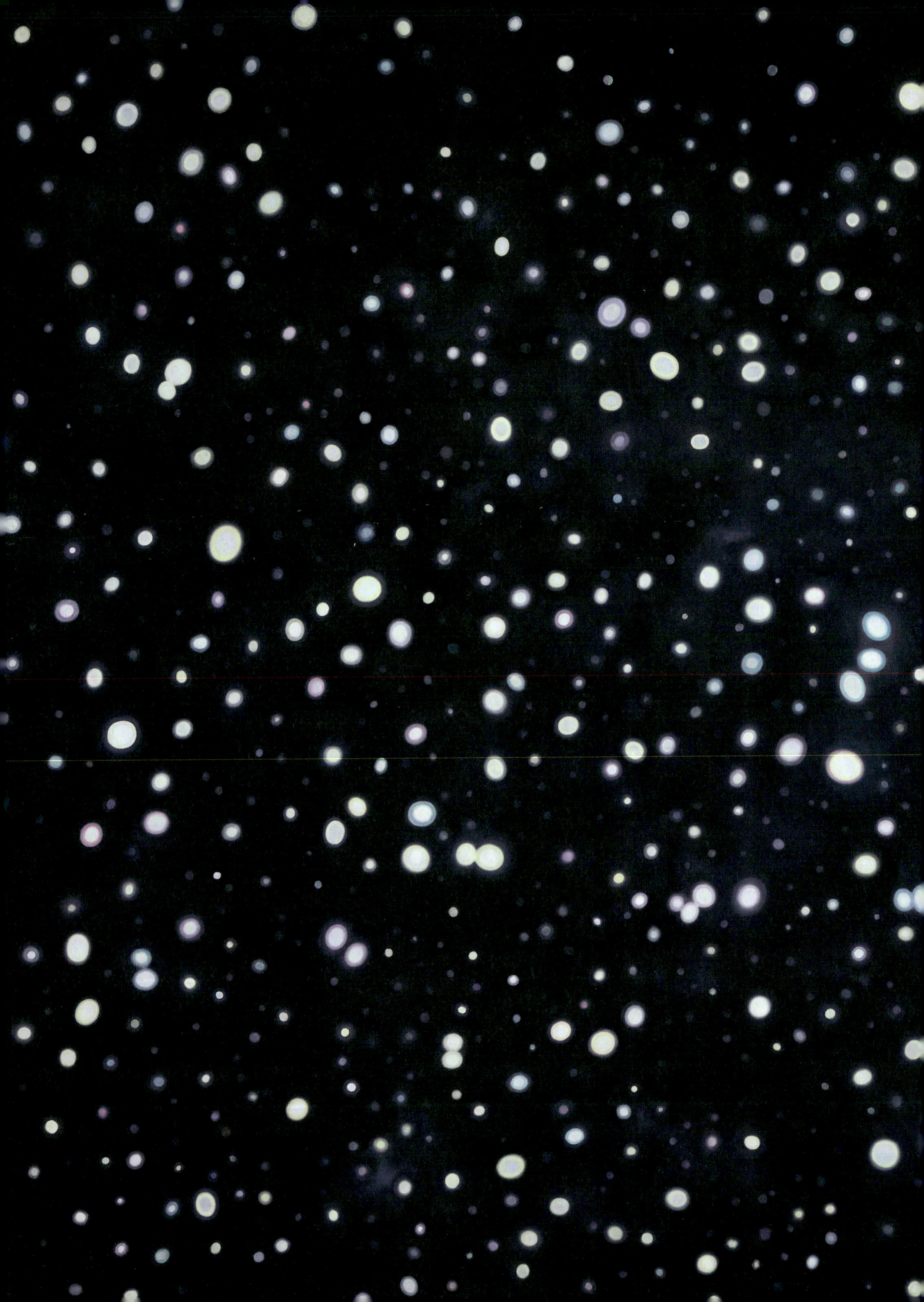

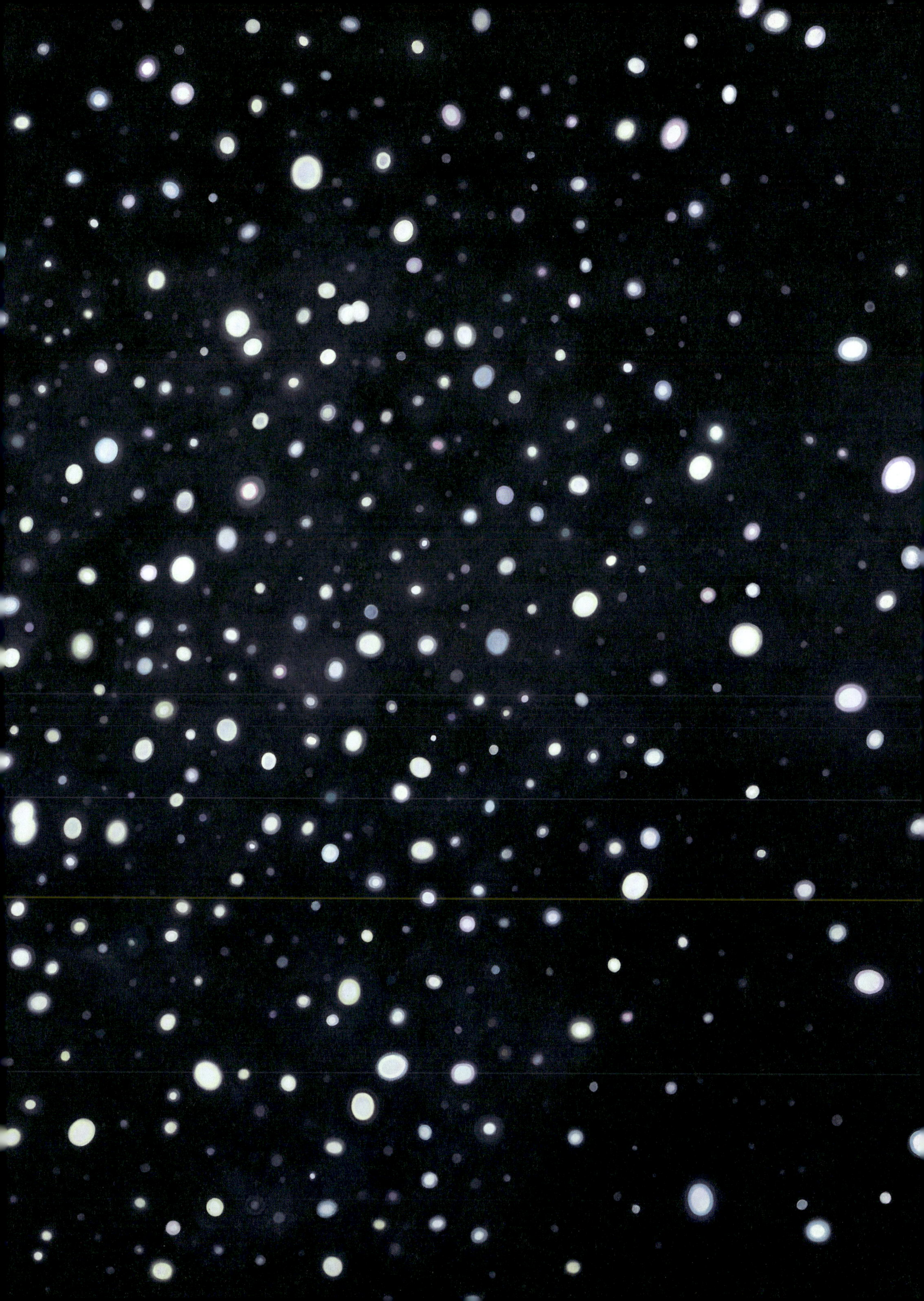

MENTAL SPACES

KRISTINE BILKAU

The sun had not yet risen. The sea was indistinguishable from the sky, except that the sea was slightly creased as if a cloth had wrinkles in it. Gradually as the sky whitened a dark line lay on the horizon dividing the sea from the sky and the grey cloth became barred with thick strokes moving, one after another, beneath the surface, following each other, pursuing each other, perpetually.[1]

These lines open Virginia Woolf's novel *The Waves*, and they sound as though Woolf was describing the *Ocean* paintings by Miwa Ogasawara. Inversely, when I look at these paintings, in which the sea touches the sky and the waves with their sharp contours almost seem to move, they make Woolf's words resonate once more, provide them with a resonance chamber, a mental space that expands and expands. Painting resembles writing, writing resembles painting, both of them a process through which we attempt to grasp the moment—with our means—in all of its complexity, fragility, and grandeur. This is the question that I continually ponder in my work as a writer, even if it is not always present in me: How do you find expression for a present that is always interwoven with memories, hopes, and wishes with a foreboding of loss and transience?

"Don't worry. You will have the richness of your thoughts," my mother told me during one of our last conversations. In those days she seldom left the house, her heart had become too weak. I was worried and felt a quiet sadness; to me she seemed cut off from the

GEDANKENRÄUME

Die Sonne war noch nicht aufgegangen. Meer und Himmel ließen sich nicht unterscheiden, nur daß das Meer leicht gefältelt war wie ein zerknittertes Tuch. Allmählich, während der Himmel weiß wurde, erstreckte sich eine dunkle Linie am Horizont, die das Meer vom Himmel trennte, und das graue Tuch wurde von dicken Streifen durchzogen, die sich, einer nach dem anderen, unter der Oberfläche bewegten, einander folgend, einander jagend, immerzu.[1]

Mit diesen Zeilen beginnt Virginia Woolfs Roman Die Wellen, *und es ist, als würde Woolf die* Ocean-*Bilder von Miwa Ogasawara beschreiben – und umgekehrt, betrachte ich diese Bilder, auf denen das Meer den Himmel berührt und die Wellen mit ihren feinen Konturen sich fast zu bewegen scheinen, bringen sie Woolfs Worte noch einmal zum Klingen, geben ihnen einen Resonanzraum, einen Gedankenraum, der sich weitet und weitet. Malen ist wie Schreiben, Schreiben ist wie Malen, beides ein Prozess, durch den wir – mit unseren Mitteln – den Augenblick, in all seiner Komplexität, Brüchigkeit und Größe, festzuhalten versuchen. Das ist die Frage, um die ich während meiner Arbeit als Schriftstellerin durchweg kreise, selbst wenn ich sie mir nicht ständig ins Bewusstsein rufe: Wie findet man Ausdruck für eine Gegenwart, die immer auch durchwoben ist von Erinnerungen, Hoffnungen und Wünschen, einer Ahnung von Verlust und Vergänglichkeit?*

»Mach dir keine Sorgen. Du wirst den Reichtum deiner Gedanken haben«, sagte

思考空間

クリスティーネ·ビルカウ

「日はまだ昇っていなかった。海に皺のある布のように小さなひだがあること以外には、空と海との区別はなかった。徐々に、空が白んでいくにつれ、空と海を分ける黒い線が地平線に現れてきた。灰色の布は太い縞状になって海面下で次々とうねりだした。あとからあとへと追いうちをかけながら、絶えることなく。」[1]

ヴァージニア·ウルフの小説『波』の冒頭である。この数行はまるでウルフが小笠原美環の描いた海の絵を描写しているかのようだ。またその逆に、海が空に触れ、繊細な輪郭からなる波がまるで動いているかのように見える時、これらの絵はウルフの言葉が響き渡り広がり続けるひとつの共鳴空間、ひとつの思考空間をもたらす。描くことは書くことのようで、書くことは描くことのようだ。その両方ともが、それぞれの方法で、すべての瞬間を、複雑性や脆さや大きさの中で捉えようと試みるひとつのプロセスだ。作家として仕事をしている間、常に意識していなくても、私はずっとこの問いに思いを巡らせている。思い出、希望、願望、喪失や、はかなさの予感が織り混ざる現在を、どうしたら表現できるのだろうか。

「心配しなくても大丈夫。あなたは豊かな思考を持つようになるから。」母は最後の会話のひとつで私にこう言った。その頃はもう、母は家から出ることも殆どなかった。心臓がすっかり弱っていた。私は母のことが心配で、ひっそりと哀しみを感じた。母は外の世界から切り離されているようだった。会話の中で「どんな気持ちなの。行動範囲がこんなに狭くなって、毎日、正直に言ってどんな気持ちでいるの」と私は彼女に聞いた。私は歳をとることと、孤独に不安を抱いていた。でも母の言葉は私を安心させてくれた。豊かな思考を持つ人は、常に十分な食べ物や水がある島に生きている。豊かな思考を持つ人は、内面に常に新しくなる大きな世界をもつことができる。それは美しいもの、悲しいもの、神秘的なもの、儚いもの、尽きないもの、それらすべてを内包する世界だ。

world. During our talk I asked her, "How does it feel? Be honest with me, how does it feel day after day, when your scope of activities has become so small?" I was afraid of old age, of loneliness. Yet her answer reassured me. "Whoever is rich in thoughts lives as though on an island, possesses a great inner world constantly renewing itself, one that has everything in it, the beautiful, the sad, the mysterious, the fleeting, and the permanent."

My mother's words fuse with Miwa Ogasawara's paintings miraculously, for in her paintings I encounter them again, these expansive mental spaces: the gaze upwards in an agitated sky with birds, some of which fade into the gray. Drops of rain that capture the light. Foaming waves that crash on a beach. A diffuse landscape, like one that flies by during a train ride, the sun low on the horizon, a day draws to its end—or is just beginning. Miwa Ogasawara's paintings speak of this, of how complex a single moment can be, a moment in which everything flows, our sensations and expectations, our memories. "The moment was all; the moment was enough," writes Virginia Woolf in *The Waves*. Everything counts, every small detail can shine and have meaning through our observation.

Miwa Ogasawara's paintings are full of a special silence: they speak of pausing, yet at the same time they bring to life the shimmering impressions of the immediate present. Even the rapid tempo at which our world today pulses is perceivable. I look at the landscape passing by me, with the delicate outlines of trees and the feeble light of the tired winter sun amid the masses of clouds. In it I recognize both the speed of our high-tech world and the quietly flowing, inward-directed perception, for which a journey in a train compartment offers space. The word *daydream* crosses my mind, for the interplay of being in the middle of it all and at the same time feeling outside. Thoughts, sensations, and yearnings are expressed; suddenly, I grasp it: a single moment of perception always revolves around the whole as well, around our

meine Mutter zu mir, in einem unserer letzten Gespräche. Damals ging sie nur noch selten vor die Tür, ihr Herz war zu geschwächt. Ich machte mir Sorgen und spürte eine leise Trauer, sie schien mir wie abgeschnitten von der Welt. In unserem Gespräch fragte ich sie: »Wie fühlt es sich an? Sag es ehrlich, wie fühlt es sich Tag für Tag an, wenn der Handlungsradius so klein geworden ist?« Ich fürchtete mich vor dem Alter, vor der Einsamkeit. Doch ihre Antwort gab mir Zuversicht. Wer reich an Gedanken ist, lebt wie auf einer Insel, auf der es immer genug Nahrung und Wasser gibt. Wer reich an Gedanken ist, besitzt eine große, innere, sich immer wieder erneuernde Welt, die alles in sich trägt, das Schöne, das Traurige, das Geheimnisvolle, das Flüchtige, das Bleibende.

Auf wundersame Weise verbinden sich die Worte meiner Mutter mit den Bildern von Miwa Ogasawara, denn in ihren Bildern finde ich sie wieder, diese weitläufigen Gedankenräume: der Blick hoch in einen unruhigen Wolkenhimmel, darin Vögel, von denen sich einige im Grau verlieren. Regentropfen, in denen sich das Licht fängt. Schäumende Wellen, die sich an einem Strand brechen. Eine diffuse Landschaft, wie sie an uns während einer Bahnfahrt vorbeizieht, die Sonne steht tief am Himmel, ein Tag neigt sich seinem Ende zu – oder er bricht gerade an. Miwa Ogasawaras Bilder erzählen davon, wie vielschichtig ein einziger Moment sein kann, ein Augenblick, in den alles hineinfließt, unsere Empfindungen und Erwartungen, unsere Erinnerungen. »The moment was all; the moment was enough«, schreibt Virginia Woolf in Die Wellen. *Alles zählt, jedes Detail, jede Kleinigkeit kann leuchten und von Bedeutung sein, durch unsere Betrachtung.*

Miwa Ogasawaras Bilder sind von einer besonderen Stille, sie erzählen vom Innehalten, doch zugleich lassen sie die flirrenden Eindrücke der unmittelbaren Gegenwart lebendig werden. Selbst das hohe Tempo, in welchem der Takt unserer heutigen Welt schlägt, ist spürbar. Ich betrachte das Bild

母の言葉は、驚くほど不思議に小笠原美環の絵に繋がっている。彼女の絵の中に私が広々とした思考空間を再び見つけるからだ。不穏な雲の空を見上げる、そこには鳥が飛び交い、そのいくつかは灰色の背景に消えて行く。光が受け止められた雨しずく。浜辺に砕け散る波の泡立ち。茫洋とした風景、電車の車外を走り過ぎる景色のようで、太陽は空低く、日が暮れていくーあるいはちょうど明けようしている。小笠原美環の絵は、私たちの情感や期待、私たちの思い出、それらのすべてが注ぎ込むある一瞬、そのひとつの瞬間がどれほど多層的でありうるかを物語る。「瞬間がすべてだった。瞬間は満ち足りていた」と、ヴァージニア·ウルフは「波」に書いている。すべてが重要で、どんな細部も些細なことも私たちの観察によって輝きを帯び、意味を持つことができる。

小笠原美環の絵画には特有の静けさがある。それは静止について語り、それと同時に、目の当たりの現在の揺らめく印象を生き生きとさせるものだ。私たちが生きている今日の脈打つ世界の速度をさえも感じさせる。私は走り過ぎる風景に、樹木の繊細な輪郭と雲間に浮かぶ冬の太陽の淡い光を見る。私はそこに高度に技術化の進んだ世界の速度と、列車の車室で心の内側に向けられ静かに流れ行く知覚の、両方を認識する。出来事の中にいるのに同時に外にいるように感じる相互作用から、白昼夢という言葉が思い出される。もしこれらの絵に人物が見られなくても、小笠原美環はそこに人がいることを感じさせる。思考、情感、憧れが表現され、突然、把握される。知覚される一瞬は、私たちの存在、愛し愛される私たち、喪失感を抱き、時には安心感を持つ私たち、絶えずそれらすべてを中心に展開している。

「日は沈んだ。空と海との区別がつかなかった。砕ける波の白い扇は波打際を越えて押し寄せ、白い影を響きのよい空洞に送りこみ、それから吐息をつきながら磯辺から引き下がっていった。」[2]

母が亡くなって数週間たった頃、私は母の居間のソファに座り母の音楽を聴き、母の本を読んだ。私は安らぎを感じ、母が思考の世界の話で何を言おうとしたのかがわかるようになってきた。歳月、蓄積された印象と思い出、それらが一緒になって、母は外界のすべてと結びついているという気持ちを持てたのだ。海辺に立って始まりも終わりもない波の動きを見つめたり、私たちが想像でこの海を思い描き、ある一日のことを、打ち寄せる波のことを思い出す時、あるいはすべての印象を呼び覚ますような美術作品を鑑賞する時、トランジションは流動的である。哲学

existence, around us, those we love, or feel loved by, lost or protected.

Now the sun had sunk. Sky and sea were indistinguishable. The waves breaking spread their white fans far out over the shore, sent white shadows into the recesses of sonorous caves and then rolled back sighing over the shingle.[2]

A few weeks after my mother died, I sat in her living room, on her sofa, heard her music and read her books. I felt protected, and I began to understand what she had meant during our conversation by her world of thoughts. The lived years, the store of impressions and memories, all that together gave her the feeling of being connected with everything outside. Whether we stand at the sea and watch the movement of the waves, which have no beginning and no end, or whether we imagine it, the sea, and recall a certain day, there, at the breakers, or whether we look at a work of art that triggers all these impressions—the transitions are fluid. The philosopher, psychologist, and Harvard professor William James wrote at the end of the nineteenth century about the vital necessity of resonance. We need—as much as the air we breathe—that we are seen, heard, and recognized by another person. James was concerned primarily with social ties, but the idea of resonance can be spun further, as we all know; it can apply to painting, music, literature, to any type of art. Just like the reader awakens a novel to life through their perception, so an observer awakens a painting to life. And vice versa: the painting touches something in us, something that was buried or forgotten. I can feel recognized and comforted by another person, and also by an artwork.

When I look at Miwa Ogasawara's series *Weltbild* (World Picture), I look into the breadth of the universe, which is filled with lights, with stars, glimmering and inaccessible. Then I sense the insurmountable isolation that each one of us bears. A form of loneliness that begins in the first months of life in *einer an mir vorbeiziehenden Landschaft mit den feinen Umrissen der Bäume und dem schwachen Licht einer wintermüden Sonne zwischen den Wolkenmassen, und ich erkenne darin beides, die Geschwindigkeit der hochtechnisierten Welt und die ruhig fließende, nach innen gerichtete Wahrnehmung, für die eine Fahrt in einem Zugabteil Raum bietet. Der Begriff* Wachträumen *kommt mir in den Sinn, für das Zusammenspiel, mittendrin zu sein und sich zugleich wie außerhalb zu fühlen. Auch wenn Menschen auf diesen Bildern nicht zu sehen sind, lässt Miwa Ogasawara ihre Anwesenheit spürbar werden. Gedanken, Empfindungen und Sehnsüchte kommen zum Ausdruck, und auf einmal wird begreifbar: Ein einziger Moment der Wahrnehmung dreht sich immer auch ums Ganze, um unser Dasein, um uns, die wir lieben, geliebt werden, uns verloren oder aufgehoben fühlen.*

Nun war die Sonne untergegangen. Himmel und Meer waren einander nicht zu unterscheiden. Die sich brechenden Wellen breiteten ihre weißen Fächer weit über das Ufer, sandten weiße Schatten in die Vertiefungen klangvoller Höhlen und rollten dann seufzend den Kieselstrand zurück.[2]

Als ich einige Wochen nachdem meine Mutter verstorben war in ihrem Wohnzimmer saß, auf ihrem Sofa, hörte ich ihre Musik und las in ihren Büchern. Ich fühlte mich aufgehoben und ich begann zu verstehen, was sie im Gespräch über ihre Gedankenwelten gemeint hatte. Die gelebten Jahre, der Vorrat an Eindrücken und Erinnerungen, das zusammen gab ihr das Gefühl, mit allem da draußen verbunden zu sein. Ob wir am Meer stehen und den Bewegungen der Wellen zuschauen, die keinen Anfang und kein Ende haben, oder ob wir es uns vorstellen, dieses Meer, und uns an einen bestimmten Tag erinnern, dort, an der Brandung, oder ob wir ein Kunstwerk betrachten, das alle Eindrücke wachruft – die Übergänge sind fließend. Der Philosoph, Psychologe und Harvard-Professor William James schrieb gegen Ende des

者で心理学者のハーヴァード大学教授ウィリアム·ジェームズは19世紀の終わり頃、人間は生きる上で共鳴を必要とすると著述した。呼吸するのに空気が必要であるように、私たちは他人から見られ聞かれ認識されることを必要としている。ジェームズはそれを主に私たちの社会的な繋がりに関連させているのだが、共鳴という考えを広げれば、私たち皆が知っているようにそれは絵画、音楽、文学や、どんな種類の芸術にもあてはまる。読む人に知覚されることで小説に命がふきこまれるように、見る人は絵に生命を与え目覚めさせる。その逆に、絵は私たちの中に隠されていたり、忘れられていた何かに触れる。私は誰か人からだけでなく、ある芸術作品によっても認識され慰めを感じることができる。

私は小笠原美環のシリーズ *Weltbild*(世界画)に、ほのめく光や星に満ちた到達することのできない遠い宇宙の広がりを見る。そして私たちそれぞれが抱える克服できない孤独に想いを寄せる。孤独のある形態、それは生命の最初の数ヶ月を羊水の中で隔離されて過ごすことで始まり、行動範囲が狭まる老年期と死で終わりを遂げる。人間であることと存在することに伴う状態。おぼろげな光を見つめるとき、私たち自身がこの光のようなもので、浮き漂いながら接近し合い、離れ離れになり、周りを巡り、瞬間触れ合いながらも、ひとりひとりでいるのが見えてくる。小笠原美環の絵は、ふたりの人間のあいだの空間、私とあなたのあいだの場所を見えるものにする。

「なぜ私が書き、なぜ私が生きているのか、それは同じこと。私は何をするべきかを見つけようとしているのだから。この奇妙な惑星で。」[3] と、詩人のザラ·キルシュは書いている。何が私たちを支え、私たちを動かし続けているのだろう。私にはそれは繋がりへの尽きない探求と憧れ、またはウィリアム·ジェームズが書いているように、共鳴を求める心だと思える。共鳴を尽きることのなく望む心、それを私は確信している。その希望は常に新たに満たされて行く。外に出られなくなった心臓の弱った女にとってもまた。愛する人を通して、私たちの心に触れて響くある女性の詩人の言葉を通して、儚く揺らめく現代や私たちの存在の美しさと壊れやすさを捉える、小笠原美環の一枚の絵を通して。その絵は私の思考空間だ。

註1 ヴァージニア·ウルフ『波』、初版:Hogarth Press, London, 1931
註2 同上
註3 Sarah Kirsch, *Kommt der Schnee im Sturm geflogen* (雪が嵐の中を飛んでくる), DVA, 2005年, 14頁

the seclusion of the uterus and ends in the unrelenting, ever narrowing scope of action of aging and dying. A state inherent to our being human, to our existence. I regard the blurred lights and see that we too are like these lights; we drift toward one another, move away from one another, circle one another, touch each other briefly and yet each one of us remains on their own. Miwa Ogasawara's paintings make the space that occurs between two persons visible, the place between you and me.

"Why I write, why I live, merges into one another. Because I want to find out what I am doing here. On this strange planet," says the poet Sarah Kirsch.[3] What is it that bears us, that keeps us moving? I believe it is the incessant search and yearning for attachment, or as William James wrote, the need for resonance. And, of this I am convinced, the inexhaustible hope for resonance. A hope that can always be rekindled. For a woman with a weak heart as well, who can no longer leave her home. Through people that we love; through the language of a poet, that makes something in us resound; through a painting by Miwa Ogasawara that captures the fragile, shimmering present, the beauty and frailty of our existence. The painting is my mental space.

1 Virginia Woolf, *The Waves* (London: Hogarth Press, 1960), 5 (first published London, 1931).
2 Ibid., 197.
3 Sarah Kirsch, *Kommt der Schnee im Sturm geflogen* (Munich: DVA, 2005), 14.

19. Jahrhunderts über die Lebensnotwendigkeit von Resonanz: Wir bräuchten es, wie die Luft zum Atmen, dass wir von einer anderen Person gesehen, gehört und erkannt werden. James beschäftigte sich dabei vor allem mit unseren sozialen Bindungen, doch die Idee von Resonanz, das wissen wir alle, lässt sich auch weiter denken, sie kann für die Malerei, Musik, Literatur, für jegliche Art von Kunst gelten. So wie die Leserin und der Leser einen Roman zum Leben wecken, durch ihre Wahrnehmung, so weckt auch die Betrachterin oder der Betrachter ein Bild zum Leben. Und anders herum, rührt das Bild an etwas in uns, das verborgen oder vergessen war. Ich kann mich nicht nur von einem anderen Menschen erkannt und getröstet fühlen, sondern auch von einem Kunstwerk.

Wenn ich Miwa Ogasawaras Reihe Weltbild *ansehe, blicke ich in die Weite des Universums, das erfüllt ist von Lichtern, von Sternen, schimmernd und unerreichbar. Dabei fühle ich mich an die unüberwindbare Isoliertheit erinnert, die jeder von uns in sich trägt. Eine Form der Einsamkeit, die in den ersten Lebensmonaten in der Abgeschiedenheit einer Fruchtblase beginnt und in dem unaufhaltsam enger werdenden Handlungsradius des Alterns und Sterbens endet. Ein Zustand, der zu unserem Menschsein, zu unserem Dasein gehört. Ich betrachte die verschwommenen Lichter und sehe, dass wir selbst wie diese Lichter sind, wir driften aufeinander zu, bewegen uns voneinander weg, kreisen umeinander, berühren uns kurz, und doch bleibt jeder für sich. Miwa Ogasawaras Bilder lassen den Raum, der sich zwischen zwei Menschen befindet, sichtbar werden; der Ort zwischen dir und mir.*

»Weshalb ich schreibe, weshalb ich lebe, fällt ja zusammen. Weil ich herausfinden will, was ich hier soll. Auf diesem seltsamen Planeten«, so die Dichterin Sarah Kirsch.[3] Was ist es, das uns trägt, das uns in Bewegung hält? Ich glaube, es ist die unablässige Suche und Sehnsucht nach Verbundenheit, oder, wie William James schrieb, das Bedürfnis nach Resonanz. Und, davon bin ich überzeugt, die unerschöpfliche Hoffnung auf Resonanz. Eine Hoffnung, die sich immer aufs Neue erfüllen kann. Auch für eine herzschwache Frau, die nicht mehr vor die Tür gehen kann. Durch Menschen, die wir lieben; durch die Sprache einer Dichterin, die etwas in uns zum Klingen bringt; durch ein Bild von Miwa Ogasawara, das die brüchige, flirrende Gegenwart einfängt, die Schönheit und Zerbrechlichkeit unseres Daseins. Das Bild ist mein Gedankenraum.

1 *Virginia Woolf,* Die Wellen, *Hogarth Press, London 1931[1], hier: S. FISCHER Verlag GmbH, Frankfurt a. M. 1992, S. 7.*
2 *Ebd., S. 233.*
3 *Sarah Kirsch,* Kommt der Schnee im Sturm geflogen, *DVA, München 2005, S. 14.*

pp. 102/103 *19.22* / 2019
38 × 53 cm / Ink on paper

p. 107 *20.06* / detail / 2020
50 × 65 cm / Ink on paper

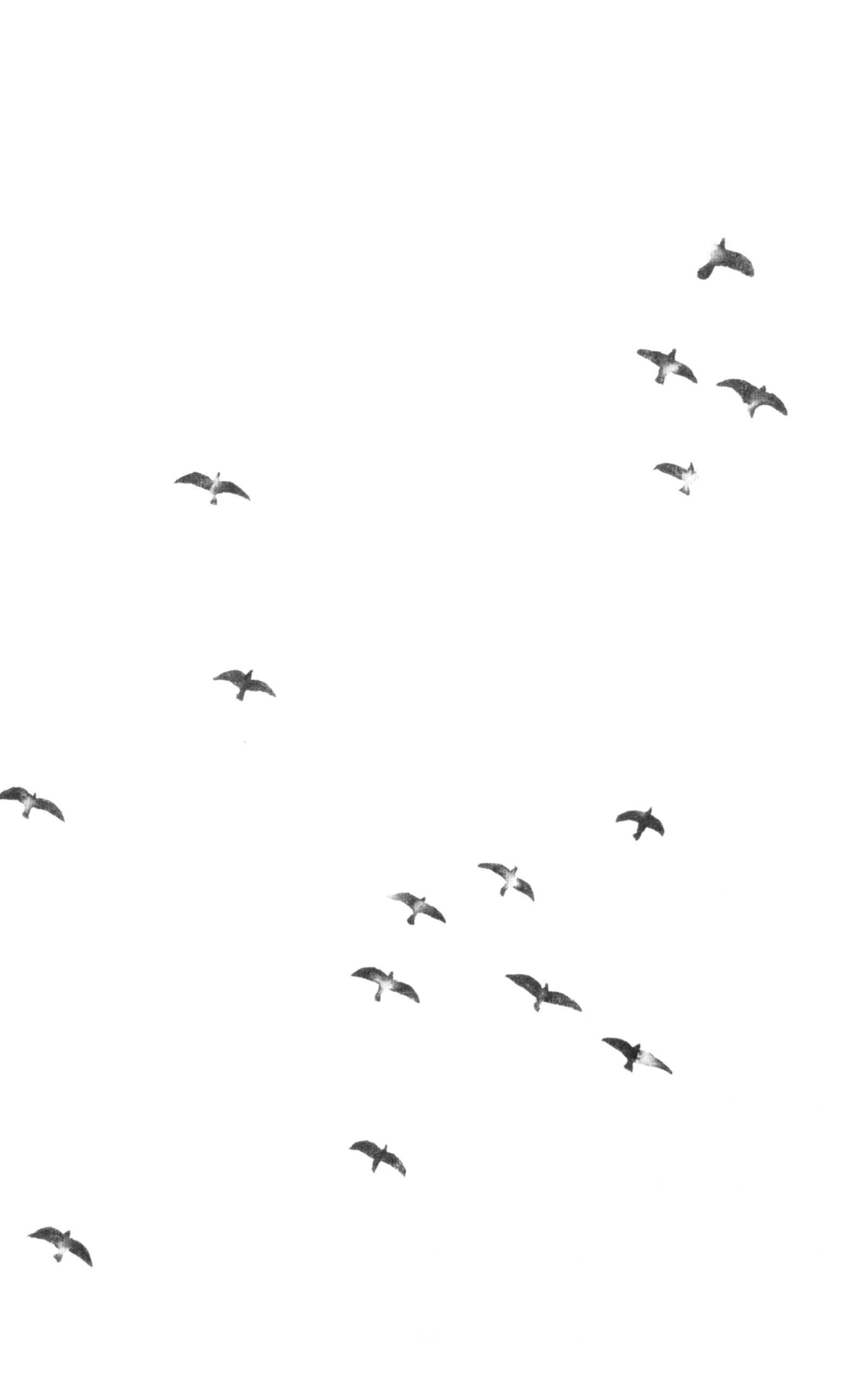

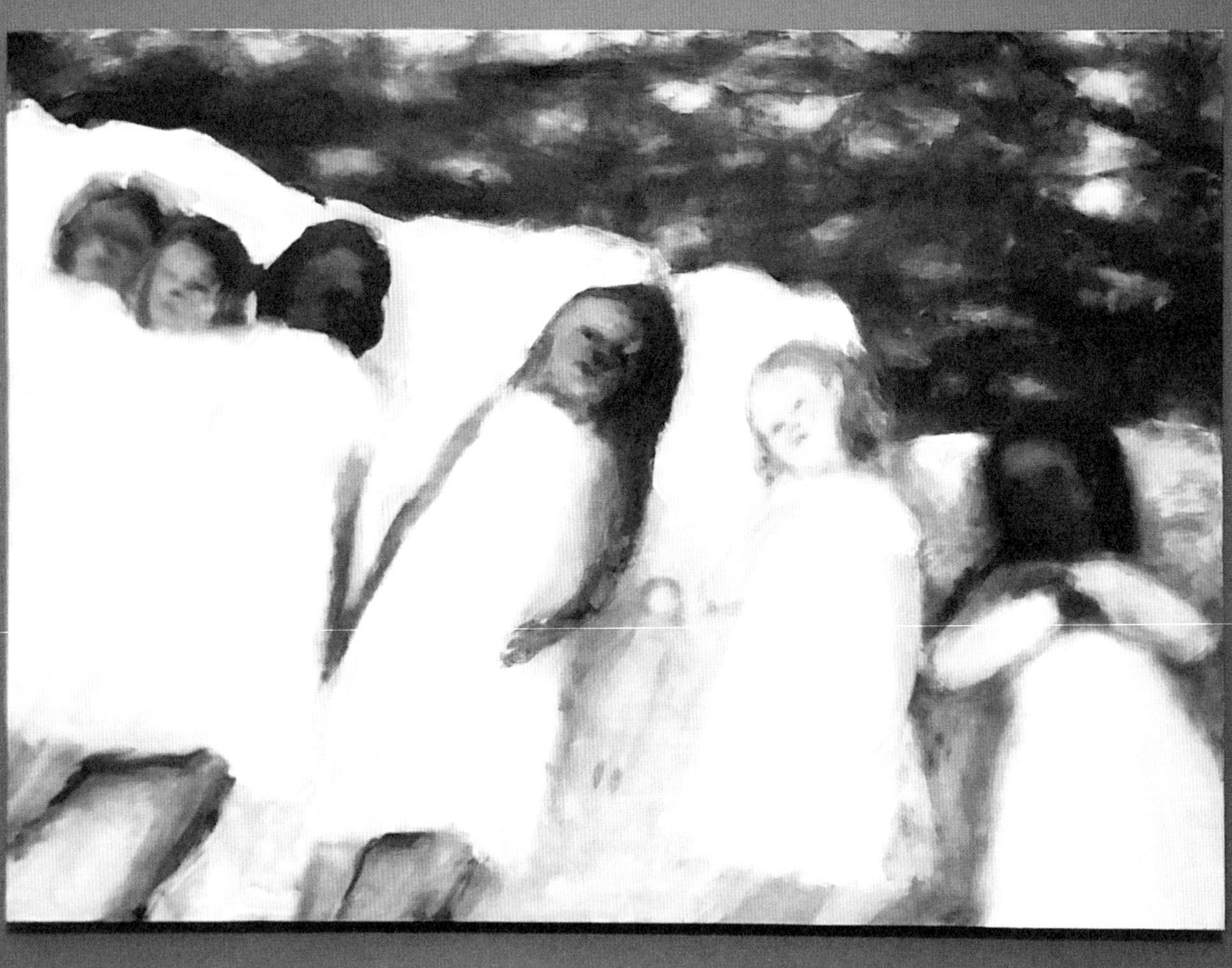

 Exhibition view *Feeling* / 2019 / Pinakothek der Moderne / Munich

MIWA OGASAWARA

Miwa Ogasawara was born in 1973 in Kyoto, Japan. In 1991 she moved from Los Angeles, where she lived from 1989, to Germany. She studied at the Academy of Fine Arts in Hamburg under Norbert Schwontkowski, Werner Büttner, and Michael Diers from 2004 to 2007. She previously studied design at the University of Applied Sciences, Hamburg, from 1997 to 2002. She lives and works in Hamburg, Germany.

GRANTS AND AWARDS

2019 Exhibition scholarship, Sparkassen-Kulturstiftung Stormarn // 2014 Exhibition scholarship, Cafe Royal Cultural Foundation // 2011 Scholarship, Japanese Government Overseas Study Program for Artists // 2008 Work scholarship, Else Heiliger Fund of the Konrad-Adenauer-Stiftung // 2006 Travel grant, German Academic Exchange Service (DAAD) // 2005 Achievement scholarship for foreign students at HfbK

SELECTED SOLO EXHIBITIONS

2020 *Figur im Raum*, Konrad-Adenauer-Stiftung in B-Part Exhibition, Berlin / *Picturing*, Galerie im Marstall, Ahrensburg // 2019 *Still*, LOOCK Galerie, Berlin // 2018 *Kowaremono*, MAHO KUBOTA GALLERY, Tokyo // 2014 *Im Licht*, Galerie Vera Munro, Hamburg // 2013 *Beyond silence*, SCAI THE BATHHOUSE, Tokyo // 2011 *New Works*, Galerie Vera Munro, Hamburg // 2010 *Hikarikage*, 1223 Gendai Kaiga, Tokyo / *ANATOMIE*, Konrad-Adenauer-Stiftung, Berlin // 2009 *Windhauch*, Galerie Vera Munro, Hamburg // 2008 *Hitorigoto*, SCAI THE BATHHOUSE, Tokyo / *Lob des Schattens*, Konrad-Adenauer-Stiftung, Berlin // 2007 *Nachhall*, Galerie Vera Munro, Hamburg // 2006 *Wem vertrauen*, plan b - kunstraum, Hamburg

SELECTED GROUP EXHIBITIONS

2019 *FEELINGS*, Pinakothek der Moderne, Munich // 2017 *Creating Space*, BMW Stiftung Herbert Quandt, Berlin // 2015 *10×10*, Konrad-Adenauer-Stiftung, Berlin // 2014 *The mysterious device was moving forward*, Longhouse Projects, New York / *Kunstepedemie – Büttner & Scolari*, Feinkunst Krüger, Hamburg // 2013 *ANKOMMEN KUNSTWERK*, Sammlung Alison & Peter W. Klein, Eberdingen-Nussdorf / *Nur Hier*, Sammlung zeitgenössischer Kunst der Bundesrepublik Deutschland, Bundeskunsthalle, Bonn / *10th DOMANI The Art of Tomorrow*, National Art Center, Tokyo // 2010 *HIGH IDEALS & CRAZY DREAMS*, Galerie Vera Munro, Hamburg / *ARTISTES FEMMES de 1905 à nos jours*, Centre Pompidou, Paris / *ANATOMIE*, Konrad-Adenauer-Stiftung, Berlin // 2009 *Twinism*, Kunsthaus, Hamburg, and AD&A Gallery, Osaka // 2008 *EIN ÜBERBLICK*, Konrad-Adenauer-Stiftung, Berlin // 2007 *5–7–5*, Kunsthaus, Hamburg / *Eleven Masters from Hamburg*, The German Ambassador's Residence, London / *Lebe wohl*, Kunsthaus Hamburg / *Diplomausstellung in der HfbK*, Hamburg / *Gestern, Heute, Übermorgen*, Westwerk, Hamburg // 2006 *INDEX06*, Kunsthaus, Hamburg / *ALLES IM FLUSS*, Altonaer Museum, Hamburg / *Plattform#3*, Kunstverein, Hannover / *top to bottom end to end*, Magazin der ÖBB, Vienna // 2005 *INDEX05*, Kunsthaus, Hamburg / *Potenziell Wandernde*, Galerie der HfbK, Hamburg / *Ehemalige Klasse Gudjonsdottir*, Westwerk, Hamburg

COLLECTIONS (SHORT LIST)

Centre Pompidou, Paris / Sammlung zeitgenössischer Kunst der Bundesrepublik Deutschland / Jil Sander Collection, Hamburg / Burger Collection, Zurich/Hong Kong / 1223 Gendaikaiga — Contemporary Painting Collection, Tokyo / ARARIO MUSEUM, Seoul

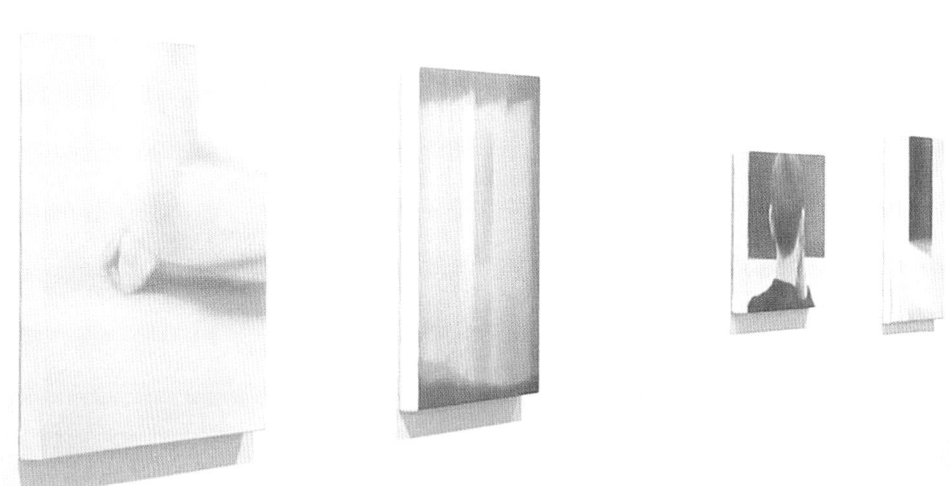

Exhibition view *Kowaremoro* / 2018 / MAHO KUBOTA GALLERY / Tokyo

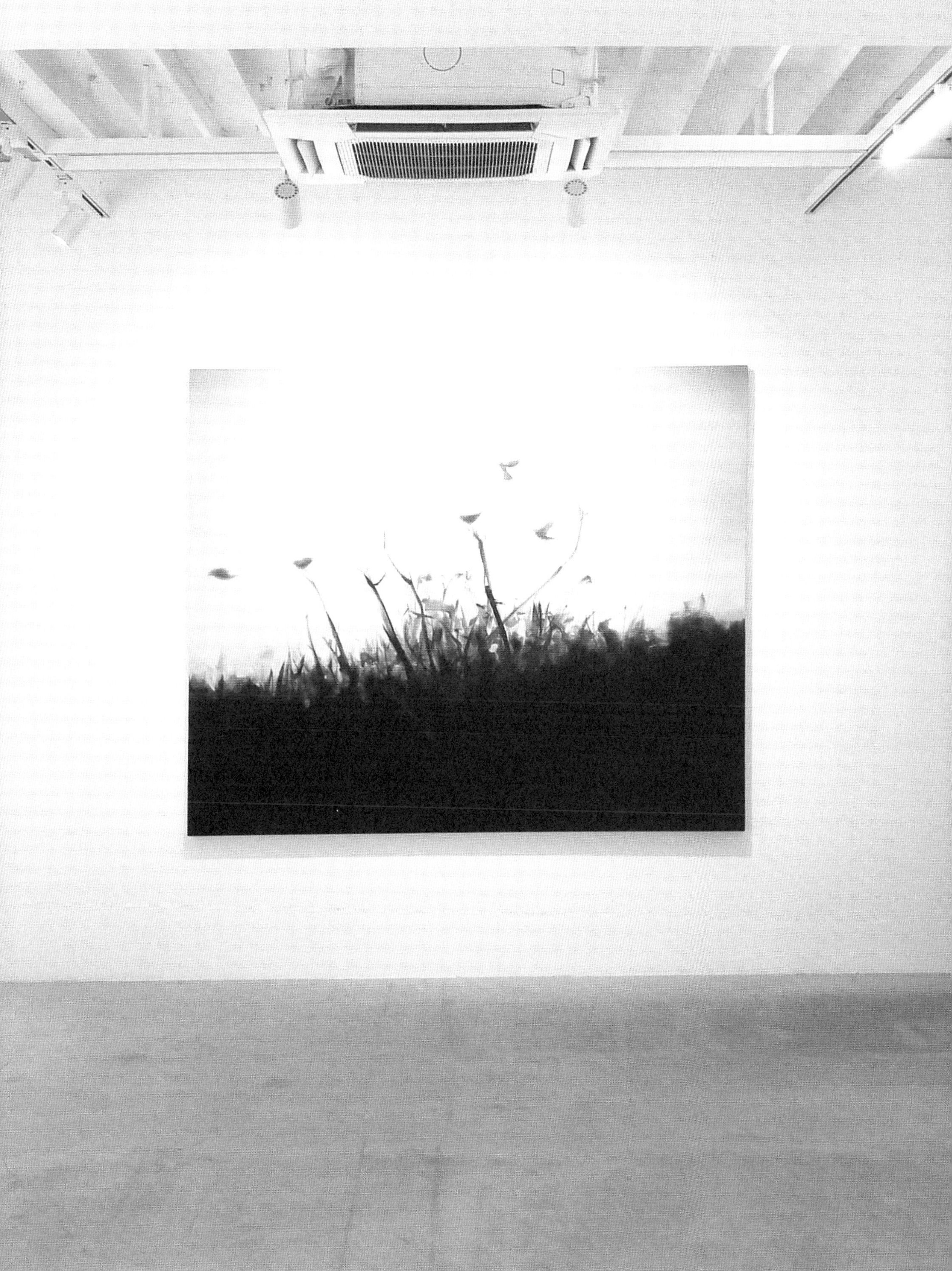

NICOLA GRAEF

Nicola Graef is the CEO of Lona·media film production company, a documentary director and a journalist. She is also a freelance writer and curator. After studying German literature, theater studies and philosophy in Munich, Paris, and London, Nicola Graef spent two years in London working freelance for the ARD and ZDF. Back in Germany, she continued journalistic activities with the NDR in Hamburg as editor and reporter with NDR television, focusing on cultural and political topics and programs. She then began working freelance, establishing the film production company Lona·media with Susanne Brand in 2001. Since then the company has produced more than 100 documentaries including portraits, series, and long feature films. As a director she has realized, for example, *Ich.Immendorff; Neo Rauch: Gefährten und Begleiter; Kirsten Heisig: Tod einer Richterin; Ma Vie: Siri Hustvedt; William Kentridge: South Africa and the Revolution;* and *Berlin: A Lonely City*. The productions of Lona·media have received numerous national and international awards. Simultaneously, she ran a private arts space for four years in Hamburg, Kunstraum plan b, and hosted a 90-minute live talk show on social and cultural topics for WDR Television. She has curated exhibitions such as *Queensize* at Me Collectors Room in Berlin; and *FEELINGS Kunst und Emotion* in the Pinakothek der Moderne, Munich, in 2019. She lives and works in Berlin.

SAYAKO MIZUTA

Sayako Mizuta works as a freelance curator, project manager, and coordinator for contemporary art exhibitions and festivals. Her curated exhibitions include *MONOKATARI — Beyond Words* (Hillside Forum, 2019); *Alterspace: Constantly Changing Temporary Artspace* (Asahi Art Square, 2014), and *Skin & Map: The Study of Body and Sense by Four Artists* (Aichi Art Center, 2010). She has run the Little Barrel project room in Omori, Tokyo (http://littlebarrel.net).

KRISTINE BILKAU

Kristine Bilkau was born in 1974. She is a writer and journalist. She studied history and literature at Hamburg University and Tulane University, New Orleans. Her debut novel *Die Glücklichen* (The Happy Ones) about an urban family getting into the turmoils of financial crisis was awarded best debut novel of the year 2015 with the Klaus-Michael-Kühne-Preis and the Franz-Tumler-Literaturpreis, and was translated into various languages. Her second novel, *Eine Liebe, in Gedanken* (A Love in Thoughts), about a young couple in the early 1960s trying to escape the repressions of German postwar society, came out in 2018. Kristine Bilkau lives with her family in Hamburg and is currently working on her third novel.

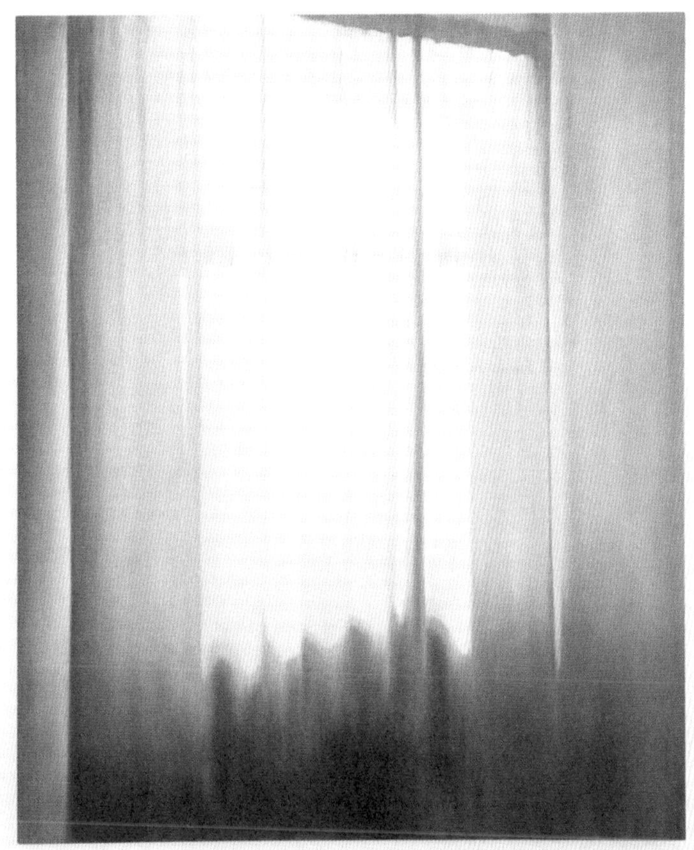

Exhibition view *Still* / 2019 / LOOCK Galerie / Berlin

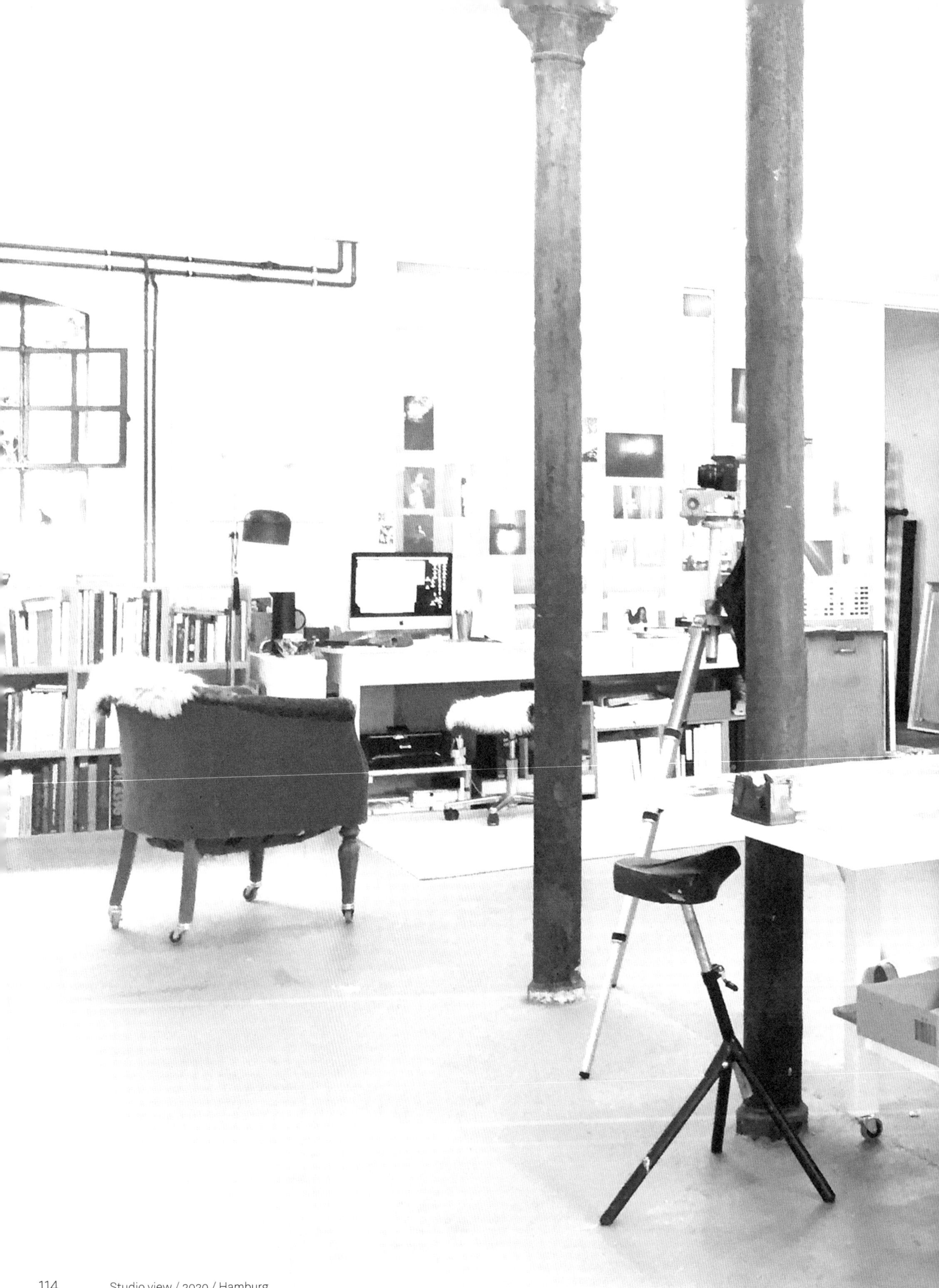

Studio view / 2020 / Hamburg

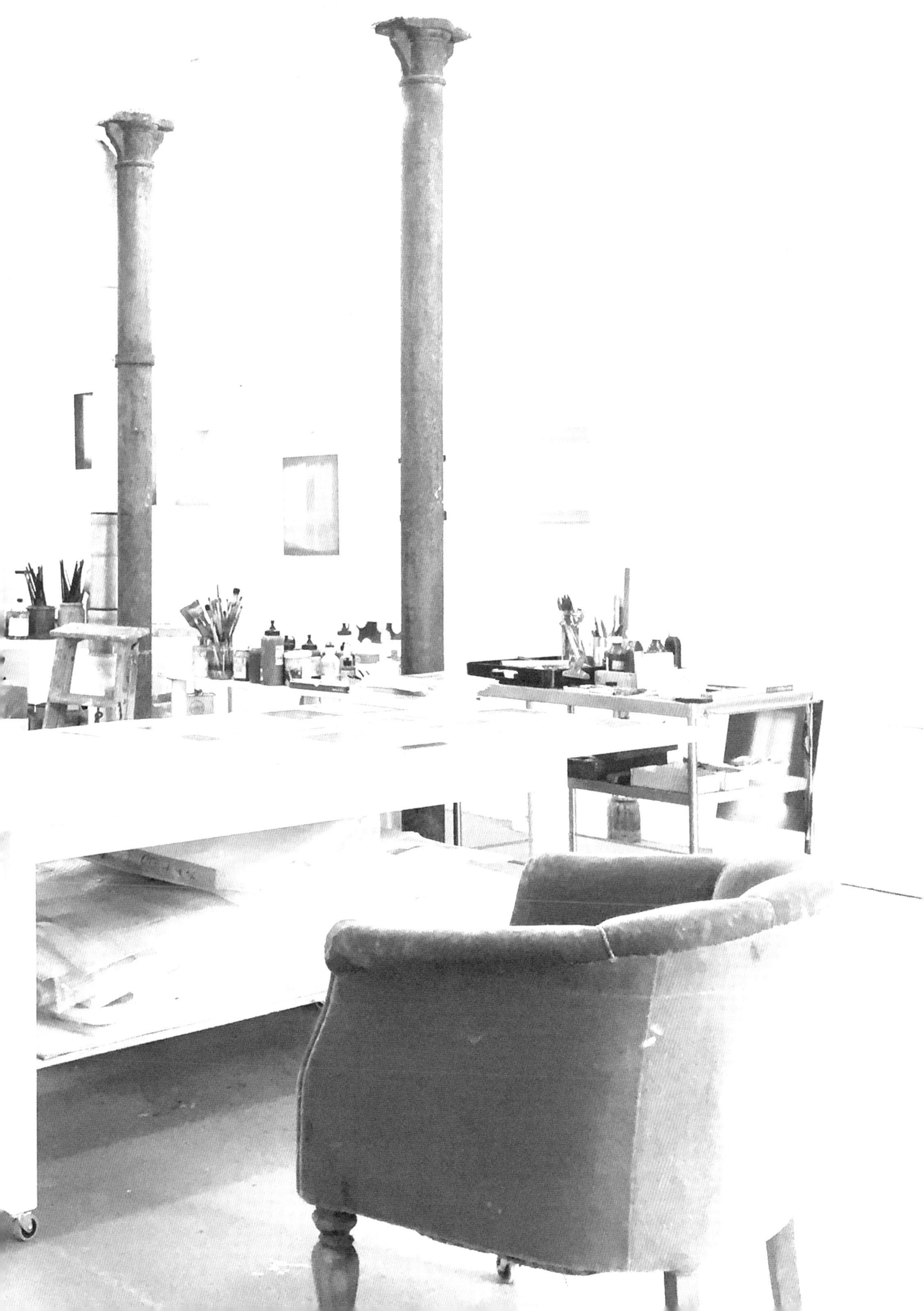

IMPRINT

PUBLISHED BY
Hirmer Verlag GmbH
Bayerstrasse 57–59
80636 Munich
Germany

AUTHORS
Kristine Bilkau
Nicola Graef
Sayako Mizuta

ENGLISH TRANSLATION
David Sánchez
Andreas Stuhlmann

GERMAN TRANSLATION
Nora Bierich

JAPANESE TRANSLATION
Nanae Suzuki

COPY EDITING & PROOFREADING
Alexander Langkals (German)
Keonaona Peterson (English)
Yumiko Urae (Japanese)

DESIGN, LAYOUT AND TYPESETTING
Vera Rammelmeyer, mischen

HIRMER PROJECT MANAGEMENT
Rainer Arnold

PRINTING AND BINDING
Westermann Druck Zwickau

PAPER
80 g/m² Blocker Perfect White (Lakepaper)
135 g/m² Magno Volume

TYPEFACE
Equitan Sans
Mplus 1p

Cover: *Raum 7*, detail, 2014, 40×35 cm
Quote, p. 2: Siri Hustvedt, *The Shaking Woman or A History of My Nerves* (New York: Henry Holt and Company, 2010)

Printed in Germany

THIS PUBLICATION IS SUPPORTED BY
EHF2010 der Konrad-Adenauer-Stiftung
Hamburgische Kulturstiftung:
»Kunst kennt keinen Shutdown«
PArt-Fonds der Spiegelberger Stiftung

SPECIAL THANKS GO TO
Rainer Arnold
Kristine Bilkau
Hans-Jörg Clement
Nicola Graef
MAHO KUBOTA GALLERY
LOOCK Galerie
Sayako Mizuta
Vera Rammelmeyer
Nanae Suzuki
Axel Winckler
Thomas Zuhr

WITH HEARTFELT THANKS TO
Hirokata, Yoko and Naoka

BIBLIOGRAPHIC INFORMATION
published by the Deutsche Nationalbibliothek

The Deutsche Nationalbibliothek lists this publication in the Deutsche Nationalbibliografie; detailed bibliographic data is available on the Internet at http://www.dnb.de

ISBN 978-3-7774-3717-0

www.hirmerpublishers.com